Ethics of AI in Art

The Future of Creativity in an AI-Driven World

Javed S.K

2

TABLE OF CONTENTS

First Edition: 2026

Written by: Javed S.k

About the Author

Javed S.k is an artist, educator, and creative professional with over 15 years of experience in art and design. Known for his strong foundation in traditional art and his evolving interest in digital creativity, he has guided many students in developing their artistic skills, particularly in drawing and visual expression.

Alongside his work as an art teacher, Javed has explored graphic design, book creation, and visual storytelling. His passion lies in combining creativity with modern technology, helping learners adapt to changing artistic landscapes.

In *Ethics of AI in Art*, he brings together his artistic background and growing interest in artificial intelligence to explore one of the most important questions of our time — how technology is shaping creativity, and what it means for artists and society.

Through this work, Javed aims to encourage thoughtful discussion about fairness, originality, and the future of art in an AI-driven world.

Dedication

This book is dedicated to all artists —
those who create with their hands, their hearts, and their imagination.

To every learner who struggles, practices, and grows,
and to those who believe that creativity is more than just a skill — it is a voice.

I also dedicate this work to my family,
for their constant support, patience, and encouragement throughout my journey.

And to the future generation of creators,
who will shape a world where technology and human creativity exist in balance.

Acknowledgement

I would like to express my sincere gratitude to everyone who supported me in the completion of this book.

First and foremost, I thank my family for their constant encouragement, patience, and belief in my work. Their support has been my greatest strength throughout this journey.

I am also grateful to my students, whose curiosity and creativity continue to inspire me every day. Teaching and learning alongside them has played an important role in shaping my perspective on art and education.

I would like to acknowledge the broader artistic and academic communities, whose discussions and ideas around creativity and technology have influenced this work. Their contributions have helped me explore the deeper ethical questions surrounding artificial intelligence and art.

Finally, I thank all the readers of this book. Your interest in understanding the relationship between AI and creativity is what makes this conversation meaningful and relevant.

This book would not have been possible without the support and inspiration of all these individuals.

Preface

Art has always been a reflection of human thought, emotion, and experience. For centuries, it has evolved through new tools, new mediums, and new ideas. Today, we stand at the edge of another transformation — one driven not by human hands alone, but by machines capable of generating images, styles, and concepts within seconds.

Generative Artificial Intelligence has changed the way we create, learn, and think about art. What once required years of practice can now be achieved through a simple text prompt. This shift has opened new doors, making creativity more accessible than ever before. At the same time, it has raised important questions that cannot be ignored.

Is this true creativity, or a simulation of it?
Is accessibility enough to call something fair?
And most importantly — what happens to the artists behind the data that powers these systems?

This book does not aim to reject technology, nor does it blindly celebrate it. Instead, it takes a step back and asks a deeper question: **Are we building a future where creativity is shared, respected, and fair for everyone?**

Through this journey, the book explores the ethical side of AI in art — focusing on issues of bias, ownership, consent, and inclusion. It challenges common assumptions and invites readers to think critically about the tools we are beginning to rely on.

This is not just a book about technology.
It is a book about people, creativity, and the choices we make as a society.

The future of art is being shaped today — and understanding it is the first step toward shaping it responsibly.

SUMMARY

In recent years, Generative Artificial Intelligence (GenAI) has transformed the way we think about art. With the release of tools like DALL-E 2, Midjourney, and Stable Diffusion around 2022, creating visual content from simple text prompts has become surprisingly easy. What once required years of practice can now be done in seconds. Because of this, many people have started to believe that AI is "democratizing" art — making it accessible to everyone.

At first glance, this idea sounds exciting. The thought that anyone, regardless of skill or background, can create art feels like a step toward equality. However, when we look deeper, the reality becomes more complex. Simply making something easier does not necessarily make it fair or truly inclusive.

For any technology to genuinely democratize an activity like art, it must satisfy certain basic conditions. In this discussion, three essential principles are considered: fair accessibility, respect for autonomy, and inclusive design.

The first condition, fair accessibility, means that a tool should reduce barriers without introducing new forms of inequality. While GenAI tools appear to open doors, they are built on datasets that often carry biases. These biases are not only present but sometimes amplified in the generated images. As a result, instead of creating equal opportunities, these systems can reinforce existing imbalances.

The second condition, respect for autonomy, is even more critical. A truly democratizing system must respect the rights, permission, and creative ownership of those already involved in the field — in this case, artists. However, many AI models are trained using artworks without the knowledge or permission of the original creators. This raises serious ethical concerns. When an artist's work is used without credit, permission, or compensation, it disconnects the art from its meaning and the creator from their creation.

The third condition, design inclusion, focuses on how these technologies are developed. If a tool is meant to benefit everyone, then those who may be affected by it — especially artists — should have a voice in its creation. Unfortunately, many AI systems are built and released without meaningful involvement from these stakeholders. This lack of inclusion increases the risk of harm and misunderstanding.

When we understand GenAI through these three principles, it becomes clear that the claim of "democratizing art" is not as straightforward as it seems. While these tools offer new possibilities, they also introduce new challenges that cannot be ignored.

In the end, true democratization is not just about access — it is about fairness, respect, and inclusion. Without these, even the most advanced technology can fall short of its promise.

CHAPTER 0: INTRODUCTION

1. In September 2022, something unusual caught the attention of the art world. An image titled "Theatre D'Opera Spatial" won first place in the digital art category at the Colorado State Fair. At first, it appeared to be a routine victory — just another talented artist being recognized for their work. However, the moment its creator, Jason Allen, revealed that the image had been generated using an AI tool called Midjourney, the narrative quickly changed.

2. What followed was not celebration, but controversy. Artists, critics, and observers across the globe began questioning the fairness of the competition. Was it appropriate for an AI-generated image to compete alongside works created through human effort, skill, and experience? Yet, the debate did not remain limited to the competition itself. It soon expanded into deeper ethical concerns about the very process through which such images are created.

3. Generative AI systems are trained on massive datasets, which include artworks, photographs, and designs collected from across the internet. A significant portion of this material is used without the knowledge or permission of the original creators. This raises serious questions about permission, ownership, and artistic autonomy. If an artist's work is used to train a machine without their approval, can the outcome truly be considered fair or ethically justified?

4. Alongside these concerns, another issue began to surface — bias. Researchers and critics pointed out that AI-generated outputs often mirror the biases present in their training data. Rather than producing neutral or universally inclusive content, these systems can unintentionally reinforce stereotypes and existing inequalities.

5. Despite these criticisms, supporters of AI technology present a very different perspective. Many within the tech industry and academic

circles argue that tools like Midjourney represent a breakthrough in creative accessibility. By removing the need for traditional artistic skills or years of training, these tools allow virtually anyone to create visual content. From this viewpoint, AI is seen as a force that is "democratizing" art — opening creative opportunities to a much wider audience.

6. While this argument is undeniably appealing, it requires careful examination.

7. This book challenges that optimistic narrative. It explains that Generative AI image tools do not genuinely democratize art-making. In fact, the claim itself can be misleading. For any technology to truly "democratize" an activity like art, it must satisfy certain fundamental conditions. At a minimum, three key principles must be fulfilled…

8. To understand whether a technology can truly be called "democratizing," it is essential to look beyond surface-level benefits and understand the principles it stands on. Simply making a process faster or easier is not enough. True democratization requires fairness, respect, and thoughtful inclusion.

9. The first principle is fair accessibility. A genuinely democratizing tool should reduce barriers to participation, making it easier for people from different backgrounds to engage in the activity. However, this access must not come at the cost of creating new forms of exclusion. If a system opens doors for some while quietly disadvantaging others — especially marginalized communities or existing practitioners — it cannot be considered truly fair. Accessibility must be balanced, not selective.

10. The second principle is respect for autonomy. Any tool that claims to expand participation must respect the rights, permission, and creative ownership of those already involved in the field. In the context of art, this means acknowledging the work, identity, and agency of artists.

Their creations should not be used, altered, or repurposed without meaningful permission. A system that ignores the voices and rights of its contributors undermines the very foundation of ethical participation.

11. The third principle is design inclusion. Technologies do not exist in isolation — they are shaped by the people who build them. For a tool to be truly inclusive, it must involve the voices of those who are most affected by it. This includes not only developers and companies, but also artists, communities, and individuals who may experience its impact directly. Without this involvement, there is a risk of creating systems that unintentionally cause harm or overlook important perspectives.

12. Together, these three principles form a basic framework for evaluating whether a technology genuinely supports democratization. Without meeting these conditions, the claim of making something "accessible to all" remains incomplete and, in many cases, misleading.

It is important to recognize that the principle of design inclusion does not stand entirely separate from the other two conditions. In many ways, it overlaps with both fair accessibility and respect for autonomy, acting as a safeguard that helps reduce potential harm — not only to the general public but especially to marginalized communities.

By involving relevant stakeholders during the development process, this condition plays a crucial role in ensuring that a tool is fair and respectful before it reaches the public. It allows creators to identify possible risks, biases, or unintended consequences early on, rather than addressing them after harm has already been done. In this sense, design inclusion becomes a proactive step toward achieving genuine democratization.

At the same time, this principle does not demand that every stakeholder must actively participate, nor does it require a fixed level of involvement. Instead, the responsibility lies with the creators of the technology. They must make a sincere effort to consider those who may be affected and provide meaningful opportunities for feedback during the development phase.

In other words, inclusion is not about forcing participation — it is about creating space for it. A tool cannot claim to serve everyone if it is built without listening to those it may impact the most. By acknowledging and incorporating diverse perspectives early in the process, the chances of creating a fair, respectful, and truly accessible system are significantly improved.

When judged against these three principles, it becomes clear that Generative AI image tools, in their current form, fall short of genuinely democratizing art. As this book explores in detail, the issue is not simply about access, but about the quality and fairness of that access.

Rather than creating a balanced and inclusive space for artistic participation, these systems often introduce new inequalities. The accessibility they offer is uneven, and in many cases, it comes at the cost of reinforcing existing social and cultural biases. Instead of reducing barriers in a meaningful way, they risk deepening the very divisions they appear to overcome.

Equally concerning is the question of artistic autonomy. By relying on data sourced from artists without proper permission, recognition, or compensation, these systems challenge the rights and dignity of creators. Art is not merely data — it carries intention, identity, and meaning. When this connection is ignored, the ethical foundation of the technology becomes questionable.

For these reasons, it can be argued that Generative AI image tools are ethically problematic, particularly because they fail to meet the essential conditions required for true democratization. These conditions are not optional — they represent the minimum standards needed for any system claiming to expand participation in a fair and responsible way.

As a result, the widely repeated claim that such technologies are "democratizing art" becomes misleading. Without satisfying these foundational principles, the promise of democratization remains incomplete, and in some cases, deceptive.

Through this discussion, this book aims to contribute to the growing conversation around the ethics of AI in art. More importantly, it seeks to challenge and critically understand the assumption that technological advancement automatically leads to fairness and inclusivity.

I will begin by exploring what GenAI image generators are and limit the scope of this book. Then, in chapter one, I will define "democratization", outlining its use through a basic understanding, and explore how the term is being used within Silicon Valley. Finally, chapters two and three will defend the conditions for legitimate democratization.

1. What are Generative AI Image Generators?

Generative Artificial Intelligence (GenAI) images — which are often casually referred to online as "AI art" — are digital visuals created through advanced text-to-image systems. These systems work by taking a written prompt and transforming it into a visual output using deep learning models. In simple terms, a user describes what they want to see, and the system generates an image based on that description.

Some of the most widely used GenAI image tools today, such as Stability AI and Midjourney, rely on massive datasets to function effectively. These datasets are largely sourced from organizations like LAION, a non-profit initiative that focuses on making large-scale machine learning data openly available. The goal behind such efforts is to support the development of AI technologies by providing access to vast amounts of visual and textual data.

The process of building these datasets is both complex and expansive. Images are collected from publicly available sources across the internet through automated systems. These images are then paired with text descriptions, often based on captions or metadata found alongside them. Over time, this results in an enormous collection of image–text pairs, which the AI uses to learn patterns, styles, and visual relationships.

To improve usability, these datasets are further organized and filtered. Factors such as image quality, resolution, and the presence of watermarks are taken into account. Some datasets are extremely large — containing hundreds of millions or even billions of image–text combinations — while others are more refined, focusing only on images that meet certain aesthetic standards.

For instance, widely used datasets include collections with hundreds of millions to billions of image-text pairs, along with more curated versions that prioritize visually appealing content. These refined datasets help AI systems produce outputs that appear more polished and aesthetically pleasing.

While this scale of data allows GenAI systems to generate highly detailed and diverse images, it also raises important questions — particularly about where this data comes from, who created it, and whether it has been used with proper permission. These concerns form a crucial part of the broader ethical discussion surrounding AI in art.

These datasets, which according to LAION were originally created to "democratize research and experimentation" (LAION, 2025c, para. 2), are becoming increasingly intertwined with GenAI image generators, with more recent datasets, such as the aforementioned LAION-5B, being funded by tech companies including Hugging Face, Doodlebot, and Stability.ai (Birhane et al., 2023). By training GenAI models on a huge quantity of images and data, they are able to use

1 OpenAI, the developer of popular GenAI image generator DALL-E and all subsequent versions, has yet to disclose exactly which dataset it used to train its model (Zhang et al., 2025).

2 LAION clarify that they “trained several lightweight models that predict the rating people gave when they were asked ‘How much do you like this image on a scale from 1 to 10?’” (LAION, 2025b). However, it’s not clear exactly who decides what qualifies as “high visual quality” and which people were used to determine the aesthetic quality of their images.

deep machine-learning algorithms to understand patterns and context within the data and create what appear to be novel outputs and images (Dee, 2024). To create a GenAI image, a human user supplies the GenAI model with a text prompt, which the model then uses to create the closest approximation it can based on the training data it has received. The more data that is fed into them, the more accurate to the inputted text prompts the outputs are, and the more “competitive” they are in their performance and on the market (Beaumont, 2022). Diffusion models are the most common type of GenAI for recent image generation, with examples including Stable Diffusion, DALL-E, Midjourney, Adobe Firefly, and Imagen. Diffusion models take existing images and diffuse them into pixels, then work to reverse the process to create new images from the static noise that mathematically corresponds most closely to a given text prompt. Their popularity comes from their ability to make high quality “original” images with high fidelity (Chen et al., 2023; Vahdat and Kreis, 2022).

The quality of the image outputs depends greatly on both the quality and quantity of the images fed into the model, where higher quality images create higher quality image outputs. Without variety and quantity, these outputs run the risk of potentially being too similar to, or replicating, the original training data (Davenport and Mittal, 2022; Zhu et al., 2024). As a result, a wide variety of images from all over the internet are used to train these GenAI models, and the need for a large volume of data requires the absence of asking permission of permission for much of the material, with Midjourney's founder David Holz stating, "there isn't really a way to get a hundred million images and know where they're coming from" (Salkowitz, 2022, paras. 14–16). The majority of GenAI image generators collect their data in this way, with only a small collection, such as Public Diffusion, claiming to train their models via an opt-in and CC0 image method of data provenance (Exline, 2024; Wiggers, 2024). This majority will be the primary focus of this book.

Defining the Scope of This Discussion

As the conversation around Generative AI continues to grow, it's important to clearly define what this book will — and will not — focus on. The world of AI-generated images is surrounded by many debates, and without setting boundaries, it's easy to lose direction.

To begin with, there is often confusion in terminology. Many companies and users casually refer to AI-generated visuals as "AI art" and the people creating prompts as "AI artists." However, in this discussion, a more careful approach is taken. Instead of calling these outputs "art," they will simply be referred to as GenAI images or AI-generated images. This distinction helps avoid unnecessary assumptions and keeps the focus on the ethical issues rather than labels.

Another common direction such discussions take is the age-old question: What is art? While this is an interesting and meaningful topic, it can quickly turn into a philosophical debate that distracts from more urgent concerns. This book does not aim to define art or decide whether AI-generated images should be considered art. Instead, it briefly acknowledges the concept only where necessary, while keeping the primary focus on ethics — especially how these systems are built and how they impact real artists.

Over the years, many researchers have explored whether machines can truly be creative or produce original work. Some argue that AI lacks human inspiration and therefore cannot create what we traditionally understand as art. While these perspectives are valuable, they are not the central concern here. The real question is not whether AI can create art, but whether the way it currently operates is ethically justified.

There are also several legal and economic debates surrounding AI-generated content. Issues such as copyright, ownership of generated images, and financial losses faced by artists are widely discussed. While these are important topics, this book is more interested in the ethical dimension rather than the legal one. Laws often take time to catch up with technology, but ethics allows us to question whether something should exist in its current form, regardless of legality.

Another area often raised is the environmental impact of AI. Training and running these models require significant amounts of energy, water, and computational resources. In some cases, generating a large number of images can have a measurable carbon footprint. While this is a serious concern and will be briefly acknowledged, it is not explored in depth here, as it deserves a dedicated discussion of its own.

Finally, there is a more subtle but important issue — the impact of AI on human skills. When people rely heavily on AI tools to create images, they may miss out on the learning, practice, and self-discovery that comes with traditional art-making. Over time, this could lead to a decline in creative skills and increased dependence on technology. However, this phenomenon is not unique to AI; similar patterns can be seen with many technologies that simplify complex tasks. For this reason, while the idea of "deskilling" is acknowledged, it is not the main focus of this discussion.

In essence, this book narrows its attention to a specific and important question:

Are Generative AI tools ethically sound, and can they truly be considered as democratizing art?

Everything else, while relevant, remains in the background — allowing us to explore this central issue with clarity and depth.

CHAPTER 1: "DEMOCRATIZATION"

1. Introduction

The idea of "democratization" is often presented as a positive and transformative force, especially in the context of new technologies. In recent years, this term has been widely used by technology companies — particularly within Silicon Valley — to describe tools that claim to make creative processes more accessible and inclusive. Generative AI image systems are frequently promoted in this way, positioned as affordable and empowering solutions that open the doors of art-making to a broader audience.

However, the meaning of "democratization" is not always as straightforward as it appears. Before accepting such claims, it is necessary to clearly define what the term actually implies in practice. Without a structured understanding, the concept risks being reduced to a marketing slogan rather than a meaningful standard.

This chapter begins by explaineding a clear framework for understanding democratization, examining both its general meaning and the way it is currently being used by technology companies. It then critically explores how this term is applied to Generative AI image tools, particularly in the context of their growing popularity.

Building on this foundation, the chapter introduces three key conditions that must be met for any technology to be considered genuinely democratizing: fair accessibility, respect for autonomy, and design inclusion. These principles will serve as the core framework for evaluating the ethical claims surrounding Generative AI in the chapters that follow.

2. Basic understanding for "Democratization"

To meaningfully understand whether Generative AI image tools are truly "democratizing" art, it is essential to first understand what we mean by democracy itself, and how the idea of democratization is being interpreted within the modern technology landscape.

The term "democracy" originates from the Greek words demos, meaning "the people," and kratos, meaning "power" or "rule." At its core, democracy refers to a system in which power rests with the people, and where individuals within a society have the ability to participate in decision-making processes. In practice, this often takes the form of representational systems, where citizens are given the opportunity to be equally represented within a structure of governance.

A defining feature of democracy is its emphasis on collective decision-making, combined with an ongoing effort to maintain a level of equality among participants. While perfect equality may be difficult to achieve, the principle itself remains central — that each individual should have a voice, and that this voice should carry weight within the system.

However, participation alone is not enough. A functioning democracy also depends on permission. This includes not only the permission of individuals in choosing those who hold power, but also the respect for the rights and choices of all participants within the system. Without permission, participation becomes hollow, and the legitimacy of the system begins to weaken.

Philosophically, democracy has often been linked to broader ideals of fairness and human flourishing. Some perspectives describe a truly democratic society as one that actively seeks to expand personal freedom and equality, allowing individuals to meaningfully engage in public and social life. From this viewpoint, democracy is not just a structure of governance, but a framework for enabling participation and inclusion.

Building on this, theories of justice emphasize that fairness must take into account those who are least advantaged. Inequalities within a system can only be justified if they ultimately benefit everyone, particularly those at the margins of society. This idea reinforces the notion that democratization is not simply about increasing access, but about doing so in a way that is equitable and just.

From a more practical perspective, democracy is also valued because it gives individuals a share of power. By allowing people to participate in decision-making, it ensures that their interests, needs, and concerns are considered. In this sense, democracy functions not only as an ideal, but also as a mechanism for balancing power and protecting collective well-being.

Understanding these foundational ideas is crucial, because they set the standard against which claims of "democratization" must be measured — especially in the context of emerging technologies like Generative AI.

While the term "democracy" comes from the "rule of the people", "democratization" has a varied and more ambiguous use. The modern use of "democratization" is primarily used by companies across a variety of different areas and industries, including in healthcare, cosmetics, finance, and app creation, for the purpose of marketing and advertising (Kelley, 2022). Democratization6, specifically through the use of AI, has become a central talking point within technology fields (Duggal, 2024; Othman, 2024; Ramos, 2024; Seger, 2023; Tuisk, 2023). In technology, "democratization" implies that certain actions and activities are made more accessible through the use of technological tools, such as the internet giving greater access to communication, and to share knowledge and information (Sadiku et al., 2020). GenAI tools are often advertised as "instruments for the democratization of artistic production" and the term "democratization" becomes synonymous, and is used interchangeably, with "accessibility" (Bak Herrie et al., 2025, p. 10). For example, "data democratization" means improved accessibility to data by minimising technical hurdles to ensure that there is "no gatekeeper...at the gateway to the data" (Marr, 2017). Companies such as Squarespace aim to "democratize good design" (The Drum, 2018, para. 2) by giving access to the masses who may lack the ability to make a website without specialised tools and assistance.

For ease of reading, due to the high number of quotes from American sources I have opted to use the American spelling of "democratization" throughout this book.

In the philosophy of technology, Feenberg (2002) connects "democratization" with the participation in activities through the tools and technology of our society. Feenberg (2002) explains how the inclusion of the majority in participation in the design of these tools is directly linked to how democratic the technology is, and can impact whether the outputs of those technologies are consistent with adequate representation and democratic values. This participation should be acknowledged in both the design of democratizing tools and in who has the opportunity to use the tool. This includes, but is not limited to, those who would be most impacted by the technology, and those who may experience greater barriers to participation in the activity that the tool is "democratizing". Therefore, if a technological tool seeks to democratize, or improve accessibility to, an activity, then it should allow opportunities for participation in ways that do not exacerbate preexisting barriers and respects the autonomy and permission of existing participants of that activity.

From these criteria, I argue that there are three minimum conditions for a technology to count as being legitimately democratizing. The first two conditions are: 1) The Fair Accessibility Condition – by aiding in reducing barriers to participation without creating new, or exacerbating existing, systemic exclusions; and 2) The Respecting artists' rights Condition – by respecting the rights and autonomy, and in particular the permission, of existing participants of the activity. For example, the invention of electronic drawing tablets improved access to art-making by streamlining the process of traditional to digital drawing, and aiding in the drawing process by removing the need (for instance) to draw a perfect circle or square. This democratized drawing as it improved accessibility without exacerbating any existing systemic exclusions, while also including digital artists in the development of the tool. While it could be argued that digital tablet creation made traditional artists feel they needed to move to digital in order to remain relevant within the art community, it didn't harm the existing participants of that activity (artists) through its creation by taking anything from them, and the art of traditional drawing was not made obsolete by the creation of drawing tablets. These two criteria will be explored in chapters two and three, respectively.

Under Feenberg's (2002) theory, technology that seeks to democratize an activity should also require a third condition; that of allowing the majority, and especially the existing participants of the targeted activity, the opportunity to be involved with the design of the technology or tool. This Design Inclusion Condition is necessary for a tool to be considered democratizing, as involving the wider public helps frame issues that could be missed, and influences the overall technology design in a way that limits harm overall (Sadiku et al., 2020). However, this condition is not exclusive to GenAI or to products with the aim of democratizing. It is instead considered a standard, or at least beneficial, within most industries that create consumer products (Li et al., 2024).

Across consumer-based products, product testing is beneficial in that it protects the public consumers but also defends the companies from damages by only rolling out products that have been subjected to quality control (Brown and Eisenhardt, 1995; Cooper and Kleinschmidt, 1987; Kleef et al., 2005). There is evidence that some products do not require consumer testing, for example in the case of product line extensions for products such as toothpaste (Dickinson & Wilby, 1997). However new products, such as artificial intelligence programs, benefit from consumer feedback, and are especially enhanced by feedback from expert and knowledgeable consumers (Schoormans et al., 1995). As a default, new consumer products of any kind, but especially technological advancements, should have a design inclusion collaboration with the people most likely to benefit from, and those most likely to be harmed by, the creation of the product. A product claiming to "democratize" adds an additional consideration of improving accessibility on top of that default. Rather than explaineding the Design Inclusion Condition as a separate chapter, it will instead be referenced throughout chapters two and three as it directly interacts with the primary conditions being explored in this book.

This does not imply that a tool or technology that doesn't claim to democratize something within society is automatically harmful to society, or that the involvement of diverse groups in the creation of a tool automatically means that it is a democratizing tool. Only when those creating the tools claim to be democratizing, or improving access, to an activity, can they be expected to meet these conditions for democratization. For example, if we take the above example of a new toothpaste line, that would not be a failure of democratization as they are not making the claim that it is a democratizing tool or technology. While it would be commendable if their product did improve accessibility to toothpaste, say through making the product more affordable than others on the market, it would not be necessary for the creation of their product based on the parameters they set for themselves. However, if they created a new toothpaste and advertised it as a tool that would "democratize" access to high quality toothpaste, or to brushing one's teeth, then that tool would be required to meet the three conditions for legitimate democratization. Failing to democratize when there is no claim of democratization is only ethically problematic if it fails to meet conditions one and two, but in cases where there are claims of democratization, the claims are also deceptive.

3. Generative AI and "Democratization"

In the case of Generative AI image tools, the idea of "democratization" is not just an abstract concept — it is a central part of how these technologies are presented to the public. The companies behind these systems actively promote them as tools designed to democratize art, creativity, and the process of artistic expression. By making such claims, they position their products within a framework that demands careful evaluation against the very principles that define true democratization.

According to publicly available statements and promotional narratives, the primary promise of these tools is to make art more accessible and affordable for a wider audience. The idea is simple and appealing: by lowering the technical and financial barriers traditionally associated with art-making, Generative AI enables more people to participate in creative practices.

Supporters of this technology — including voices from both industry and academia — argue that these tools have the potential to reshape the art world. They suggest that GenAI systems challenge explaineded hierarchies, where artistic creation has often been limited by access to training, resources, or institutional recognition. In this sense, AI is seen as a force that levels the playing field, allowing individuals without formal artistic backgrounds to produce and share visual content.

A key part of this argument rests on the belief that traditional art and design require specialized skills, tools, and materials, which may not be easily accessible to everyone. From this perspective, Generative AI removes these barriers by simplifying the creative process. Instead of years of practice or expensive resources, a simple text prompt can now generate complex and visually striking images.

While this vision of accessibility is compelling, it raises an important question: does making something easier automatically make it more fair or inclusive? This is where the earlier framework becomes essential. If Generative AI is to be understood as a democratizing force, it must be judged not just by its convenience, but by whether it truly meets the conditions of fair accessibility, respect for autonomy, and inclusive design.

Therefore, GenAI is "leveling the playing field" (Sahota, 2024) and democratizing art in an unprecedented way (Hong and Curran, 2019; Wang and Ma, 2019).

"Democratization" has become synonymous with new technology and is used frequently as a catch-all by "Big Tech" (Verdegem, 2024). It's used to imply a consideration for the people using the product and to instil confidence in consumers that these new products are made, in theory, with the public in mind (Kelley, 2022). OpenAI (2025) claims that the process of using descriptive text prompts to create images "democratizes art creation, making it accessible regardless of one's traditional art skills..." and that anyone from a "liberal-democratic country" should be cheering on "the success of OpenAI rather than 'authoritarian governments'" (Samuel, 2023, para. 2). In their FAQ section, OpenAI (2025) also claim that their image generator "democratizes art creation, making it accessible regardless of one's traditional artistic skills" and "lower(s) the barriers to entry for digital art creation". Stability.ai, the company responsible for Stable Diffusion, claims that their GenAI model is "democratizing image generation" (Stability.ai, 2022, para. 6) by "empowering billions of people to create stunning art within seconds" (Stability.ai, 2022, para. 3).

Online and in the media, the claim of AI "democratizing art" has become the calling card for defending the new technology. Some examples include: how AI will lead to the "democratization of art creation" (Filimowicz, 2024); that "AI has begun to democratize creativity" (Duggal, 2024); AI has the "ability to democratize access" to the world of art (Pixie, 2023, para. 2); "Democratized generative AI...kickstart[s] a new wave of innovation...by levelling the playing field" (Sahota, 2024, para. 1) and "helps users of any creation try out new things without fear of failing" (Sahota, 2024, para. 15). There are claims that AI has the potential to "democratize" the creative process itself (Schröter, 2020), and "democratize creativity" with "unprecedented efficiency and accessibility" (Othman, 2024, p.1). Park (2024, p. 1) suggests that if AI image generation could even extend to the "democratization of artistic expression", stating that GenAI "challenges traditional art hierarchies", makes "artistic creation accessible" by integrating "art into democratic processes" (Park, 2024, p.8).

Throughout this messaging, GenAI image generators are marketed as an accessibility tool. The primary claims focus on GenAI's ability to give creativity to all, reduce barriers to making art, and making visual creation accessible to those without the design backgrounds or skills (OpenAI, 2025; Tuisk, 2023). Accessibility plays a crucial role in modern society. Its origins are often traced back to transportation, design and land development, where access was related to geographical location and how that location may impede on an individual's ability to fully engage with certain necessary human activities, such as having access to housing, food, and work (Huskinson et al., 2024; Lau and Chiu, 2003; Pirie, 1979). A notable definition of accessibility is made by Hansen (1959, p. 73) who states that accessibility is the "potential for opportunities for interaction", particularly in relation to taking part in a particular activity or set of activities. Under these definitions, accessibility can be understood as reducing barriers and improving access, and as having two dichotomous dimensions: a spatial dimension, wherein access is related to location and geographical conditions, and an aspatial dimension, relating to socioeconomic and demographic characteristics (Ashik et al., 2020).

Digital accessibility, falling under the aspatial definition of accessibility, more specifically focuses on certain sub-groups of people, such as the disabled and elderly, and their ability to use digital technologies and navigate the internet (Petrie et al., 2015). Digital accessibility is a combination of factors, including hardware, software, training, and the user, all working harmoniously together to ensure a dynamic and inclusive product (Botelho, 2021). On this definition, one could make the argument that many of our modern tools have endeavoured to "democratize" something within society that was previously segregated to only a small sub-group of people. For example: telephones democratized quick long-distance communication; the internet democratized access to information and knowledge; and cars, bikes, and public transportation democratized transportation.

The use of AI to aid in digital accessibility is a prevalent topic of discussion, with some noting that AI has the potential to "enhance accessibility for people with disabilities" (Chemnad and Othman, 2024, p. 1). Tools and technology have offered the public many helpful opportunities to improve accessibility to those who are worse off; such as eyeglasses, canes and sidewalk indicators for the vision impaired; ramps for wheelchairs; hearing aids; text-to-speech and speech- to-text;

mobility aids; prosthetic limbs; and so on (World Health Organisation, 2024). Online, accessibility tools refer to elements in web design that aid those with disabilities in navigating and engaging with online content, such as colourblind modes, keyboard inputs, and transcripts for audio (Henry, 2024). If we take the statements made by OpenAI, Stability.AI, and Midjourney at face value (AI Art Generator, 2023; OpenAI, 2024; Stability.ai, 2022), it's safe to assume that the consensus on how we should interpret the use of "democratization" in regard to GenAI image generators is primarily a focus on improving accessibility to art-making and creativity. While authors like Seger (2023) and Seger et al. (2023) argue that we shouldn't be conflating the term "democratization" with "accessibility" due to how ambiguous a term "democratization" seems to be, ultimately the majority of AI companies use the terms interchangeably and harken it back to the ideals of "greater access" to art (Ramos, 2024, para. 5) and making art "accessible to a broader audience" (Park, 2024, p. 6).7 Therefore, with AI companies use of "democratization" being synonymous with "accessibility", and considering socioeconomic and demographic characteristics as intrinsic to accessibility, successful and legitimate democratization should prioritise inclusion and respect of all subgroups of people who may participate in the activity. Democratization should consider the potential harms that could impact marginalised and vulnerable groups through the roll-out of a technological tool. If an accessibility tool fails at reducing those demographic or systemic barriers, is also sometimes synonymous with "affordability", but then there is a contradiction as the products can often times be expensive and require an understanding of the operational context, thereby making the claims of affordability questionable (Bak Herrie et al., 2025).

and potentially aggravates pre-existing barriers within society, it would delegitimise its claim of democratization.

4. Democratizing Technology

While not having a positive or negative value in and of themselves, technology can't be understandd in a vacuum, free from the arguably antidemocratic values that are inevitably at the core of much of technology's creation (Feenberg, 2002, p. 12). Technology, or technè, are man-made artifacts where the aims of the artifact are fundamentally tied to the people who design it, but is also shaped by the people who use it and what they use it for (Franssen et al., 2024; Navarro and Hancock, 2023; Pezzano and Pavanini, 2025). In short, a democratizing technology is human-made, human focused, and should always aim to put "the people", or the "demos", first (Sadiku et al., 2020). If we were to take the concept of using artificial intelligence to "democratize" art at face value, then that would imply the need for there to be some interaction between the decisions to implement such a technology and the people who it would directly affect, both negatively and positively.

While technology, and more recently AI, has made digital art creation more accessible, for a tool like GenAI to claim to democratize art-making then it must involve the people, and to imply that GenAI will democratize art and improve accessibility implies that there should be a discussion between decision makers and the public before such a technology is rolled out, particularly with those who the new technology will be directly affecting. If we are democratizing something, then one of the most important aspects of the democratic process should be to allow for the input of all citizens, especially those who it may impact negatively. If a technology is being made for the people to allow greater access for them, then it seems prudent to be asking them if that's what they want, rather than assuming it's what they want. The decision making involved in rolling out a new technology may not be able to include a vast majority of the general population in its design or decision

making process, but at minimum it shouldn't ignore the population who will be most
directly impacted by it, or the technology risks being interpreted as profoundly undemocratic (Feenberg, 2002).

5. Chapter Conclusion

In this chapter, a clear framework for understanding democratization has been explaineded, along with an examination of how the term is currently used within the context of Generative AI. It has been shown that GenAI companies frequently present their image generators as tools that make art more accessible and affordable, positioning them as inherently beneficial to creative participation.

However, rather than accepting these claims at face value, this chapter has outlined three essential conditions that must be met for any technology to be considered genuinely democratizing: fair accessibility, respect for autonomy, and design inclusion. These principles provide a foundation for critically evaluating whether such claims hold true in practice.

The following chapters build upon this framework.

Chapter Two focuses on the Fair Accessibility Condition, arguing that Generative AI image tools, in their current form, can cause significant harm to marginalized groups. Due to the biases present in their training data — which are often reflected and even amplified in their outputs — these systems risk reinforcing harmful stereotypes and existing inequalities. As a result, rather than creating fair access, they may contribute to further imbalance.

Chapter Three understands the Respecting artists' rights Condition, highlighting how these technologies raise serious concerns regarding the rights of artists. By using artistic works without meaningful permission, recognition, or compensation, GenAI systems challenge the autonomy of creators. This chapter also addresses common defenses of AI image generation — such as arguments around artistic gatekeeping, claims of AI "inspiration," and comparisons to photography — and critically judges their limitations.

Throughout these discussions, the Design Inclusion Condition remains an underlying theme. The importance of involving affected communities in the development of such technologies is closely tied to the broader ideals of participation and permission that define true democratization.

CHAPTER 2: THE FAIR ACCESSIBILITY CONDITION

Generative AI Image Generators and the Amplification of Systemic Bias

1. Introduction

With a clear framework for democratization now explaineded, this chapter turns to the first and perhaps most fundamental condition: fair accessibility. As previously defined, a tool can only be considered genuinely democratizing if it reduces barriers to participation without creating new or deeper forms of exclusion.

This chapter explains that Generative AI image tools, in their current form, fail to meet this condition.

Although companies such as OpenAI present these technologies as tools that promote inclusivity and encourage diversity in creative expression, there is a significant gap between these claims and the reality of how these systems function. The promise of accessibility suggests a more equal and open creative space; however, the underlying structure of these tools tells a different story.

Rather than removing barriers in a meaningful way, Generative AI systems often reproduce and intensify the biases already present in their training data. These biases do not remain hidden — they are reflected and, in many cases, amplified in the images produced by the models. As a result, instead of fostering diversity, these systems risk reinforcing harmful stereotypes and deepening existing inequalities.

This chapter explores how such biases manifest across multiple dimensions. In particular, it understands the ways in which Generative AI image tools can perpetuate gender bias, racial bias, and ableism, despite being marketed as inclusive technologies. These issues highlight a critical contradiction: a system cannot claim to improve accessibility while simultaneously disadvantaging certain groups within society.

To support this argument, the chapter begins with an overview of the datasets used to train these models, focusing on how bias becomes embedded at the foundational level. It then moves on to analyze the types of stereotypes and patterns that emerge from this data, and how they translate into problematic image outputs. Finally, it considers some of the solutions that have been proposed to address these concerns, while critically evaluating their effectiveness.

Ultimately, this chapter concludes that, in its current state, Generative AI image technology does not satisfy the Fair Accessibility Condition. Instead of enabling equal participation, it risks perpetuating the very inequalities it claims to overcome.

2. An Overview of the Bias in the Training Material

Although the companies creating these GenAI image generators claim the models are impartial, there is an inherent bias to the LAION datasets being used to train these models, and these biases reflect a systemic marginalisation that is present in society. In an effort to create high fidelity images, GenAI models are trained on an enormous amount of data, and their outputs are highly dependent on the input; this includes not only what they've been trained on but also what is lacking from the training material (Corrall, 2024). Because GenAI is trained to make connections between the text descriptions of images and the images themselves, the captions and alt-text on the training data is intrinsic to the quality and accuracy of the image outputs. As humans, we cherry-pick what elements are the most important and notable to label when uploading images onto the internet, inadvertently deciding what details are worth mentioning in an image and what elements are not (Ananya, 2024; Fraser et al., 2023; Misra et al., 2016; Nudelman, 2025). Rather than offering only unbiased and objective descriptive options for the user, GenAI image models instead steer the output to one that is statistically the best fit within the training data which inevitably resembles the biased tendencies present in the inputs (Zou and Schiebinger, 2018).

The imbalance in the GenAI image outputs imply a consistent pattern of incomplete captions on the images being used to train these models. The GenAI models require detailed text prompts from users to create specific images, but in the absence of any detailed prompt, for example prompting for "a person" but lacking factors such as race, nationality, or gender, GenAI image generators output images primarily of men from Europe or North America, with the implication that the default for "personhood" within the training data, at least in the case of Stable Diffusion, is of a white man (Ghosh and Caliskan, 2023). For another example, if someone uploads an image of a white, male CEO but labelled the image as simply "CEO", then the datasets are trained to infer that "CEO" is identified as white and male. The same happens on the opposite end of the spectrum; when dark-skinned women are labelled with captions such as "maid" or "poor", then those terms become synonymous with images of black women.

When such labelling happens across millions of images, the model calculates that statistically when prompted for attributes such as poor or successful, they default to black or white respectively (Bianchi et al., 2023; Yang, 2025). The shallow nature of the captions on the collected images doesn't necessarily represent a malicious intention of the original uploader to exclude certain subgroups of people from representation. Rather, it is an example of the way that humans tend to be flawed in their descriptions, often defaulting to their singular worldview and inadvertently forgetting to include other defining characteristics of the images they upload to the internet (Ananya, 2024; Misra et al., 2016).

These flawed descriptions result in biased image outputs that encompass a litany of systemically marginalised groups within society, including race, gender, religion, culture, and body types, as well as the intersection of these classifications (Ananya, 2024; Bates, 2025; Nicoletti and Bass, 2023; Nudelman, 2025; Silva, 2023; Tiku and Chen, 2024). For example, Thomas & Thomson (2023) found instances of ageism and sexism when asking for images of job titles, finding that only young-looking people were shown for non-specialised roles, and only men were shown when asking for specialised roles. Sobey (2025) found that GenAI image generators refused to output larger or disabled bodied people unless explicitly prompted to, implying thinness and able-bodied as the status quo. Hulick (2024a) found that GenAI tended to exaggerate racial stereotypes, with prompts like "poor person" outputting only dark-skinned individuals, and "attractive person" outputting almost exclusively young, light-skinned results, most with bright blue eyes.

The bias seen in GenAI image generation is not isolated; all GenAI models trained in this fashion, including LLMs such as ChatGPT-3 and Google's Gemini, are also susceptible to racist, sexist, and homophobic outputs based on their training data (O'Hagan, 2024). This interpretation of the world under a predominantly white and masculine lens can be seen throughout much of AI development, including virtual assistants, chatbots, and portrayals of AI in fiction and media (Cave and Dihal, 2020; Leonard, 2024). While the bias present in GenAI image generation is identifiable across other AI technologies, the harm by GenAI image generation is more overt due to its visual format. GenAI image generators summarise how certain sub-groups of the societal hierarchy project their worldview onto the internet into a more literal, visual form. This means that the aesthetic worldview present in the majority of the training data, noted as being majority white, heteronormative, and masculine (Ho et al., 2025; M. West et al., 2019), is often over represented in the outputs and becomes the default when the GenAI models interpret the text prompts given by the average user.

Due to how generative AI programs are made and trained, through the high quantities of images scraped from the internet, they reflect our own systemic biases and inequalities back at us in a magnified fashion (Bates, 2025, p. 228). These models pick up what is the majority conception of the world and are trained to interpret that as being the predominant worldview, inadvertently explaineding that worldview as the international standard. This determines what worldview is presented as more "important" or "correct", further propagating what society deems as the status quo, which is reflected by the outputs of the image models. Ultimately, GenAI produces images that lack the multifaceted nature of society, leading to potentially discriminatory outputs that reinforce gender, ethnicity, and disability biases (Bianchi et al., 2023; Currie et al., 2024b; Maslej et al., 2024; Silva, 2023; Tiku and Chen, 2024). This harms already vulnerable groups and is counter-intuitive to the GenAI claims of accessibility and democratization as it fails to improve opportunities for participation in the activity of art-making without exacerbating preexisting systematic stereotypes. The next sections will explore in more detail the most identifiable harmful biases of gender, race, and disability that are present in the training material and the outputs of GenAI image generators.

2.1. The Gender and Racial Bias

The datasets that the majority of the most popular GenAI image generators, such as Midjourney, Stable Diffusion, and DALL-E, are trained on originate from Western nations, therefore reflecting the Western perspective and Western aesthetic ideologies in their data (Bendel, 2023; Maslej etal., 2024). This leads to the outputs of GenAI image generators creating stereotypes of the predominant online North American or European point of view, resulting in a hardening of a limited, and primarily white, worldview (Tiku et al., 2023). The GenAI models represent a bias towards a euro-centric, western conception on not only what art is, but also opinions on aesthetics and what should be classified as "beautiful" and "ugly" (Tiku and Chen, 2024). The most pronounced areas of underrepresentation and stereotyping are regarding the intersection between race and gender. This is an amplification of existing marginalisation of women of colour that can also been seen in other areas of AI, such as facial recognition (Birhane, 2022). Within these datasets, the western ideals of beauty are often being pedestalized and, by the time the public has the opportunity to question these ideals, they are already embedded deeply into the GenAI models in ways that are almost impossible to undo (Lavoipierre, 2024).

When the data used to train current GenAI image models does not adequately represent all groups within society, it risks over-generalising and under-serving certain sub-groups of people (UNESCO, 2024). This is especially true for women and non-white individuals, who are often minimised to a shallow depiction of reality. A high quantity of online images and photos that contain people generally represent the parts of gender identity and ethnic groups that the internet deems as "most attractive", with evidence suggesting this is highly skewed to a white-washed and reductive version of humanity (Silva, 2023). For example, when given the prompt of "beautiful woman", GenAI image generators generally present the prompter with an almost exclusively light skinned, thin, able bodied woman, and often skewed toward Anglo facial features, like small noses and double eyelids (Tiku and Chen, 2024; Yang, 2025). Bates (2025, p. 245) found that when prompting for an "American woman", Stable Diffusion primarily provides images of a Western media conception of attractive, white, thin women with long hair and airbrushed skin. When asked for "the most beautiful woman in the world", DALL-E 2 generated images of exclusively white women, all dressed in Western style clothing (Parra and Stroud, 2022). Ananya (2024) notes that white skin is considered the default within current image generators, due to white people representing a large portion of the training material, and the aforementioned lack of specificity in the captions of the training images.

Women, and especially women of colour, are also underrepresented in the outputs of GenAI image generators when depicting them in professional positions, or in positions of power and authority. When asking Stable Diffusion to produce images of people in high-paying jobs, Nicoletti and Bass (2023) found that the model produced three times as many images of men, with only low-paying jobs such as housekeeper or cashier not being dominated by a white male demographic. In another study, Currie et al. (2024a) found that when asking DALL-E 3 for generated images of medical students, the model generated 92% as men and 100% as light skinned, a statistic that did not reflect the actual number of Australian medical students (54.3% being women), but was instead a reflection of the inherit bias present in the training material. The same result could be found when asking DALL-E 3 for images of pharmacists, where despite 64% of Australian pharmacists identifying as female, the model only produced images with women 29.7% of the time and again produced zero people with darker skin tones (Currie, John & Hewis, 2024). These studies show that GenAI image generators can amplify existing race and gender biases and misrepresent the true diversity in these fields.

The biased outputs from GenAI image generators perpetuate stereotypes in a way that can seriously harm those in society that don't match the status quo. When the images of certain professionals only represent a small sub-group of people, those outside that group feel ostracised from participating, resulting in fewer diverse people training for or applying for those roles (Gisselbaek et al., 2025; Mack et al., 2024; Nicoletti and

Bass, 2023; Wenger, 2024). This is exacerbated by the number of images GenAI image generators can, and do, produce, resulting in new waves of biased images flooding the internet daily. For example, if an individual wants an artistic rendition of "a doctor" but more than 90% of the outputs are of white or Asian men, then those who don't appear within those demographics may feel they don't belong in that space, regardless of their actual skill or aspirations. The harm this causes can further intensify educational
and professional barriers for those whom the image outputs don't acknowledge, or only acknowledge via misrepresentation (Nicoletti and Bass, 2023; Nudelman, 2025). This has the potential to affect future applicants, who may feel unwelcome in these fields when they see fewer images representing them online (Gorska and Jemielniak, 2023; Kay et al., 2015).

The real-world impact for biased AI systems can be seen in cases such as Amazon's decision to scrap its AI recruitment tool; Since Amazon's AI tool had been trained predominantly on male resumes, this resulted in a bias against resumes submitted by female candidates, automatically penalising any resumes that mentioned the term "woman" in any way, or that had feminine names or descriptors (Dastin, 2018). This undermines diversity and inclusion initiatives, programs which were put in place to aid in the accessibility of non-white people to professions that require higher education, such as physicians (Lee et al., 2024). This demoralisation of marginalised groups seems to be antithetical to GenAI companies' proclamation of democratization and accessibility.

To further compound the issue of sexist outputs, the most popular training databases accumulated by LAION include vast amounts of pornography and violent imagery, including that involving children (Heikkilä, 2022a; Tiku and Chen, 2024). This results in an amplification of a hypersexual representation of women. Zhou et al. (2024) note that due to the pornographic origins of much of the training data, the models produce images of women who are predominantly depicted as submissive and men who are depicted as more dominant. For example, GenAI produces images of women who are primarily depicted as young, smiling and happy, while men are shown as being older, with neutral or even angry expressions (Zhou et al., 2024). When searching the LAION ata used to train AI, the sexual imagery is more pronounced when searching for particular ethnicities, such as Asian, Indian, or Nigerian (Birhane et al., 2021). The images that were returned were clearly sourced from pornographic websites that skewed towards fetishism of non-white cultures. Ghosh and Caliskan (2023) found that Stable Diffusion perpetuated a Western fetishisation of women of colour, specifically of women from Latin America, Egypt, Mexico and India.

This oversexualisation of women is seen in abundance when observing the more insidious areas of GenAI image and video generation. For example, in a 2019 study on Deepfake videos,8 Noel (2024) found that 96% of those deepfake videos were pornographic and nonconsensual in nature, with a 99% of those videos targeting women. This is harmful for two reasons. Firstly, the likenesses of real women are being taken without permission to create distressing images and videos that misrepresent them. With the technology becoming more and more life-like as it improves, this can cause problems in their real lives as these AI created simulations are linked with their real-life counterparts, causing emotional and sometimes physical distress, particularly if the woman dresses a certain way due to religious beliefs and is being depicted unclothed (Bates, 2025).

Secondly, when synthetic images and videos online predominantly feature women in submissive, controlled roles, and fail to represent them in roles where their autonomy, self-worth, and intelligence are respected, over time the applications that create that media have the power to subtly shape the way the that users see the real world, amplifying gender and race biases one image at a time (Bates, 2025; O'Hagan, 2024). Over time this could result in the user internalising the biases presented by the AI, subconsciously taking the prejudices present in the outputs on as their own (Wach et al., 2023; Zhu et al., 2024). This harm is compounded by the potential of having GenAI models trained on their own synthetic data, further exacerbating existing barriers for women and influencing how they are viewed within society.

The gender and racial bias present in GenAI image generation is reflected in who is using and funding this new technology. In 2019, women comprised of only 15% of all AI research staff at Facebook and 10% at Google (S. M. West et al., 2019). Studies from 2024 show that 71% of men aged 18-24 use AI weekly, compared to only 59% of women of the same age (Bates, 2025; Kohler, 2024). A more recent study shows a marked increase in female usage of ChatGPT by June 2025, with 52.4% of the user base identifying under a feminine first name (Chatterji et al., 2025). However, this study notes in the breakdown of how users are using the AI, that those with Deepfake videos are fabricated videos where an individual has their likeness used to train a model that can then create synthetic videos involving them (Birrer and Just, 2024).

masculine first names were more likely to use ChatGPT for image generation,9 while feminine named users opted for writing and practical guidance (Chatterji et al., 2025, p. 25).

In the 2024 Artificial Intelligence Index Report, Maslej et al. (2024) found that, although the proportion of gender or ethnically diverse people has increased, white men still represented the majority of workers, faculty and students within the AI and IT space in North America and Europe, with Asian men coming in second. In Europe, men continue to dominate the IT, CS and computer engineering (CE) space, with the highest proportion of female graduates being 35.2% in Bulgaria, and the lowest proportion in France at 14.8% (Maslej et al., 2024, p. 425). The CEOs of the top- ranking AI companies creating these image generators, such as OpenAI, Midjourney, Stability.AI, Ideogram AI, all identify as male (Christianson and Handcock, 2025). In the UK, female founded AI start-ups only accounted for 2.1% of venture capital deals, with female-founded AI companies raising 6 times less capital per deal than all-male founder teams, and firms with majority or simply equal representation of women at the decision maker level making up less than 5% of all venture capital firms in AI (Wajcman et al., 2023, p. 5).

These statistics aren't stated to discount the hard work that these individuals do, or to imply that their success is completely tied to their gender identity, but rather to put into perspective the disproportionate amount of impact affluent men are having on this up-and-coming technology. It has been shown that diverse teams, including a higher representation of women and people from ethnically diverse background, contribute to better innovation (Sung and Choi, 2021; Talke et al., 2010), offer valuable alternative perspectives (Moody et al., 2003), and often financially outperform companies with less diverse teams (Hunt et al., 2023). Despite the proven positives of including diversity in the design and creation of a product, GenAI image generators instead defaults to a white, male worldview. The bias present in the training material of GenAI, that is duplicated and exaggerated within the visual outputs of this technology, exacerbates the invisibility of worldviews outside of the Eurocentric male view that dominates the internet. The studies lists image generation under "multimedia" and clarifies that this involves modifying and creating images. technology that claims to democratize an activity must reduce barriers to participation without exacerbating existing systemic biases, but in an effort to democratizing art-making, GenAI images intensifies existing stereotypes of non-white people, women, and especially women of colour, by either oversexualising them, infantilising them, or degrading them, which further marginalises them within society.

2.2. Ableism and Disability

When discussing the aims for democratizing art through GenAI image generation, one of the primary arguments for its benefits is that it will ultimately help those with disabilities who would normally "lack" the physical or cognitive ability to create art and participate in art culture normally (Crowe, 2025; Mace, 2023). This is a common trend within technology discussions as digital accessibility tools are nothing new to the online space. For example, a modern accessibility tool for the visually impaired is alternative-text (alt-text), a text descriptor that's attached to a digital image explaining in detail what an image contains, which serves both as a substitute for images when they fail to load, or for reading software to pick up and recite. It also improves search engine optimisation and makes it easier for people to find certain images online, making it a tool that improves access both in finding images and for more people to view and understand them.

Some authors argue that GenAI has the potential to be an accessibility tool similar to text- to-speech technology. Heidt (2024) claims that GenAI is helpful for people identifying as disabled or neurodivergent, and uses the example of a doctoral student with aphantasia using GenAI image generators to help her visualise. In a similar case study, Glazko et al. (2023) note that an individual with aphantasia and motor impairments was able to use GenAI image generators to help her visualise passages of descriptive text in fiction novels, and uses the technology to help her generate photorealistic sketches for concept. Rappaneau (2023) notes how GenAI image generators can help artists who, due to an accident or medical incident, can no longer produce art like they used to, such as the case of artist Sean Aabera, who suffered a stroke and could no longer use his dominant hand to sketch. These are valid examples of ways in which GenAI image generators are aiding in improving accessibility to art-making, and there is no question that, despite the ethical failings of the technology, it has the potential to help people in some cases.

However, while some within the disabled community may find benefits in using GenAI image generators, the technology has an insidious implication. Although it claims to empower disabled people to create, some believe it discounts not only those that have found ways to create despite their disability, but could itself be classified as potentially ableist as some of the companies creating these models imply their image outputs are a better, more accessible way for those with disabilities to make art (Shew, 2020). Creativity and art creation have been noted as some of the few modes of expression where disability isn't necessarily a barrier to participation, and can even propel artists into making art in new and creative ways (Kirmer, 2024). Proclamations that people with disabilities can "finally" participate in art-making (Orfanides, 2025) could be interpreted as dismissive of those with disabilities who create in their own unique way, without the use of GenAI technologies. Humans have always been creating art despite their disabilities, and sometimes use their disabilities as a driving factor to make their own unique art.

On top of the ableist insinuations, GenAI misrepresents body types and disabilities in both its training material and its image outputs. Sobey (2025) notes that unless a GenAI model is explicitly asked to produce a larger or a disabled body, GenAI rarely depicts alternative bodies types outside of thin and able bodied. This harmful stereotyping can be seen in many of the outputs from Midjourney or Stability.AI when prompted to create images that include disability. For example, Glazko (2023) notes that although Midjourney is helpful for visualising fantasy or able bodied people, it presented either inaccurate or harmful stereotypes of disabled people. Mack et al. (2024) found that images including disabilities skewed towards exclusively presenting individuals in wheelchairs, which was shown as the most important element in the image. These outputs also dehumanised the subject by presenting them almost exclusively as sad or depressed (Mack et al., 2024). They also found instances where certain disability descriptors, such as "bipolar", would return error messages which explained that the image model couldn't produce the images as the prompt violated the community guidelines (Mack et al., 2024). This implied that more than simply not acknowledging those with disabilities, these models could be understood as being programmed to interpret certain disabled characteristics as offensive and refused to generate anything for them.

While this choice to not produce images with certain prompts may have been done as a safety measure to avoid exacerbating harm through the potential negative results, this avoidance of finding safe ways to include certain kinds of mental health diagnoses can further perpetuate stereotypes about certain conditions such as bipolar disorder or schizophrenia, likening them as being something that should be hidden away from "normal" depictions of society. The decision for GenAI to generate generic images, or refuse to generate any images, when prompted with certain disability or genetic descriptions harms those that are already the victim of erasure and exclusion within society, compounding their real-life experiences of feeling invisible within an able-bodied society (Sarhan and Hegelich, 2023).

The harms caused by these GenAI's models due to lack of representation also extends to positions of authority, as some image models refuse to depict someone with a disability in any kind of leadership position. When asking DALL-E or Stable Diffusion to show a disabled person leading a meeting, Bianchi et al. (2023) found that they created images with a disabled individual, mostly white and female, and usually in a wheelchair, that was listening to someone else leading, rather than leading themselves. This same problem is observed when asking for images of inclusive spaces, such as a bathroom for those with physical disabilities, where the outputs demonstrated a very limited understanding of the needs of disabled people, showing a bias in the input data towards an ableist worldview (Manzoor et al., 2024).

GenAI is the tool that many are proclaiming to "even the playing field" for art-making, making it easier for those with disabilities to create without having to worry about the "how" of their creating (Heidt, 2024; Kirmer, 2024; Occupational Therapy Australia, 2025). However, while GenAI companies claim that their technology was manufactured to improve accessibility, it's important to note that rarely is that stated with the disabled or neurodivergent in mind. When these models are being marketed as being accessible "to everyone", they are primarily concerned with artistic ability, not disability (Parthasarathy, 2023). Although GenAI companies claim to be improving accessibility to art-making, which traditionally implies a focus on disability accessibility and inclusivity, this technology is made for the able bodied person who doesn't have the time to dedicate to a creative practise, such as a banker from Hong Kong or a truck driver "who's making his own baseball cards" that David Holz, founder of Midjourney, makes direct reference to (Salkowitz, 2022, para. 24).

GenAI image generators are not made with disabled or neuro-divergent people in mind, but AI companies try to take credit for creating a tool that happens to have a beneficial side effect to some of those who identify as disabled. This is despite the companies not having equity in mind, and not including those with disabilities in the data collection or creation of AI-based systems (Mankoff et al., 2024). On the Design Inclusion Condition for legitimate democratization, a technology must enable the participation of affected sub-groups in the design of the tool to minimise the potential harms. The aid that the technology is giving to some isn't a design element, but rather a side effect to a technology that is ultimately harmful to disabled communities and doesn't explicitly consider them in the implementation of their technology, despite claiming to aid in their accessibility to art-making.

The combination of harms, including the lack of representation and consideration of the disabled community, the biased outputs of what it means to be "disabled", and the intersectionality of being a combination of marginalised groups, leads those within the disabled community to feel either invisible or stereotyped, reinforcing harmful power systems through a technology that claims to be democratizing (Jääskeläinen et al., 2025; Rodman, 2023). This further alienates them from the rest of society and perpetuates stereotypes about what it is to live in a different body than that of the "standard" depiction of white, thin, and able bodied (Mack et al., 2024). Although there are some instances where GenAI helps with accessibility, the current models fail to mitigate the harms to a group of people they are claiming this technology is improving accessibility for, ultimately minimising the good that these tools could be doing by perpetuating stereotypes and potentially ostracising anyone who isn't able bodied.

Overall, due to the lack of diversity in the training data and the perpetuation of that singular worldview in their image outputs, GenAI image generators are exacerbating societal stereotypes of vulnerable groups, amplifying bias and reinforcing an exclusionary and narrow worldview. GenAI image generators reinforce and exacerbate existing barriers that exclude certain marginalised groups within society and perpetuate systemic harms through the outputs of these programs. AI companies creating and training GenAI image generators fail to acknowledge the least advantaged in society, or enable them opportunities for design participation, and instead place new significant burdens on marginalised groups, either through exacerbating stereotypes or identity erasure. Therefore, GenAI image generators do not legitimately democratize the activity of art-making as they fail both the Fair Accessibility Condition and the Design Inclusion Condition for legitimate democratization.

3. Attempted Solutions

Some companies, such as Google, have attempted to rectify the lack of diversity in the outputs of their image generators by overcompensating with more diverse outputs. This was done by adding a diversity filter that triggered when certain prompts were used, editing the users inputted prompt and adding more detailed descriptions, such as changing "a group of rich people" to "a diverse group of elegantly dressed people" (Baum and Villasenor, 2024, emphasis added). However these images featured inaccurate or misrepresentative portrayals of certain groups due to these prompt additions being triggered at inappropriate times, such as presenting an Asian woman as a German solider in the 1940's, or a black woman as a US senator in the 1800's (Hulick, 2024a; Robertson, 2024). This inadvertently erases the history of race and gender discrimination, and instead of white washing history it injects it with false diversity, misrepresenting certain groups of people and forcing diversity into historical moments and groups that were actively hostile to them, such as depicting a black man as a Nazi (Pressler, 2024). While the intentions behind these kinds of retrospective fixes may be laudable, they ultimately fail to acknowledge the predominantly white, male culture that informs how many of these GenAI models interpret their given data. These kinds of belated solutions result in a Band-Aid fix for issues that need to be addressed from the ground up. When only addressed after the product goes to market, they risk not only exacerbating systemic exclusions, but also creating new issues through what could be labelled as 'diversity overcompensation', which results in outcomes that cause additional harm to these vulnerable communities by making them the unsuspecting target of attack from those who take these quick-fix remedies to be part of an aggressive "culture war" (Pressler, 2024; Robins- Early, 2023). This has the unfortunate implication that the fail-safes Silicon Valley tech companies may be implementing are inadequate to mitigate the harms caused by their models. In this bittersweet attempt to correct the lack of diversity, Google instead exacerbated the harm, showing that not all methods of action are automatically good simply because they include diversity. Rather, these changes amplify how disconnected these companies are from the issues, implementing blanket fixes and expecting that to be enough to heal the harm, rather than considering diverse opinions in the original design of the product.

The use of LAION datasets without oversight or supervision is negligent on the part of these companies. A dataset primarily created for research purposes should not be used to train GenAI image generators that are hastily put on the market without interventions or fail-safes. This isn't to say that we can't fix the problem, or that these companies shouldn't try to mend the harm their products are doing, but rather highlights the necessity of the Design Inclusion Condition and a need to involve the people who these problems directly affect. It's safe to assume that if more people from backgrounds outside of the what we are typically seeing from the western AI workplace culture were given the opportunity to check these fixes, or were able to test the products before they were released to the public, then they could have flagged the potential harms before any changes or overcompensation methods were implemented or even needed (Bates, 2025).

While having a more diverse workforce would not change the biased images used to train current popular GenAI image generators, it would potentially offer more points of reflection within the process, both before the product goes to public, such as questioning the training data or identifying biases outputs, and before any patches or quick fixes are implemented. Having a diverse workforce provides more opportunities for alternative viewpoints, better communication, sustainability, productivity, and profitability (Joseph et al., 2021; Lachlan-Hache et al., 2020; McCuiston et al., 2004; Saxena, 2014). For GenAI, a diverse design team would also provide more opportunities for individuals to identify when they see, or don't see, an accurate portrayal of themselves in the outputted images.

Researchers such as Birhane (2022), Zhang et al. (2025), and O'Hagan (2024) suggest that the best tool to mitigate these harms is transparency, not only of the data sets but also of the models themselves, as this would enable greater collaboration with diverse groups in the public, and would make it easier to identify any problems in the data. The general ethical consensus is that transparency and accountability in AI minimises harm, improves trust, and could benefit democratic values (Cheong, 2024; Novelli et al., 2024; Waelen, 2022). Between 2023 and 2025, Stanford University (2025) found that there was an increase in transparency from 37% to 58% across major AI model developers, which is a promising improvement. However, authors such as Buick (2025) and Matulionyte et al. (2025) argue that while beneficial, transparency would not be sufficient to address the concerns surrounding GenAI training material. Based on the ongoing biases present in GenAI image outputs, more robust improvement than just transparency is necessary to include marginalised groups in the discussion for there to be a significant change.

3. CHAPTER CONCLUSION

When people, particularly people who are already underrepresented in the media, don't see themselves in any of the GenAI image outputs, and instead only see images that represent them as the "other", and their identity being reduced to the most "acceptable" parts according to these image models, then it further ostracises them within society (Silva, 2023). In this chapter, I haveexplored how the bias present in the LAION training material, particularly that relating to gender, race, and disability, is amplified in the outputs, further perpetuating stereotypes and reinforcing existing barriers. I also argued that GenAI image generators fall short of being a tool designed for accessibility. Rather, it takes ownership of that label to reap the benefits, despite not designing the tool with disability accessibility in mind and not enabling participation of marginalised groups in the design. Therefore, GenAI image generators fail to meet both the Fair Accessibility Condition and the Design Inclusion Condition for democratization as they have not reduced the barriers to art-making without creating or exacerbating pre-existing systemic exclusions. The next chapter will explore the second condition for legitimate democratization: the Respecting artists' rights Condition, and explore the effect of GenAI image generators on artists.

Chapter 3: "The Respecting artists' rights Condition" Generative AI Image Generators fail to respect the autonomy and permission of the artists they rely on

1. Introduction

For a tool or technology to legitimately democratize an activity, I argue that they are required to respect the autonomy of the existing participants of that activity. I refer to this condition for democratization as the Respecting artists' rights Condition. The current primary stakeholders, and those that have the most to lose in the introduction and roll out of GenAI image generators, are artists (Zhang et al., 2025). Current GenAI image generators disproportionately affect artists over any other group. Just as the outputs of a technology embody the values of society (Feenberg, 2002) so too do the outputs of an artist embody their personal values (Allred and Aragon, 2023; Araya, 2023; Goetze, 2024; Jiang et al., 2023; Sullivan and McCarthy, 2007; Zhang et al., 2025). GenAI image generators don't only threaten artists livelihoods and reputations, but also violate their autonomy, and use their work without permission, credit, or compensation (Chayka, 2023; Jiang et al., 2023; Kawakami and Venkatagiri, 2024).

In this chapter, I will argue that because the companies creating the popular GenAI image generators lack any meaningful permission from the artists who are necessary for the technology to exist, they fail to respect the autonomy of the existing participants of art-making, therefore failing to meet the Respecting artists' rights Condition necessary for legitimate democratization. I will begin by exploring the core claim that GenAI image generators democratize creativity and art-making. Then, I will dissect the lack of any meaningful permission and the harm to artists, and the necessity of the Design Inclusion Condition for artists in the creation of GenAI image generators. Finally, I will explore some of the key arguments for GenAI image generators, such as artistic gatekeeping, the way GenAI image generators are "inspired" and "learn" like humans do, and the comparison of GenAI image generation to photography, and argue they are insufficient to defend current GenAI image generators.

2. The "Democratization" of Art

The primary claim made by AI companies for the creation of GenAI image generators is that art- making and creativity are inaccessible to the average person due to the required time and the skill uptake needed to create unique artworks. In their Q&A section, OpenAI (2025) states that the process of using prompts to create images “not only democratizes art creation, making it accessible regardless of one's traditional artistic skills, but it also paves the way for innovative expressions in art” and that GenAI image generators empower the user to “expand [their] creative boundaries by turning [their] written ideas into visual realities efficiently and effectively”. Stabiliity.AI (2022) state that their GenAI model is “empowering billions of people to create stunning art within seconds.” As explored in the basic understanding, Silicon Valley uses the term “democratization” synonymously with “accessibility”, claiming that GenAI “improves access” to art-making. GenAI image generators are being marketed as a means to “level the playing field for would-be artists” (Merchant, 2023). Bak Herrie et al. (2025, p. 2) argue that GenAI can facilitate users, regardless of artistic skill, to generate images and to wield two “aspects of artistic democratization”, by being both an active participant by generating images, and a passive contributor through the use of their digital images being used in the training material.

The concept of democratizing art has also been thought of as “liberating” art from the “traditional constraints of physical and skill limitations” of art-making, allowing for the realisation of “ideas that were previously unattainable” (Park, 2024, p. 5). However, this idea conflates skill limitations as being an inevitability for many people. This implies that GenAI technology has granted everyone with the freedom to create that they couldn’t have been achieved by traditional means. However, I argue that this is an exaggeration. Artistic skill, like any skill, requires time, patience and practise to realise. Art-making has been described as: a process of finding a problem and gathering information (Sawyer and Henriksen, 2024); a series of problem solving tasks (Ecker, 1963); and a process of experimentation and sustained effort (Daniel, 2022). Every successful artist, whether that success is measured monetarily or otherwise, had to go through a period of awkward, less than perfect idea realisation before becoming proficient in their chosen artform. Although we may prefer not to make mistakes as a matter of pride, to learn necessitates mistake- making, and those mistakes contribute to our ability to grow, develop and learn. Some authors, such as Chomsky et al. (2023), argue that when using AI to create outputs, rather than making with the intention of learning and creating, we may be following a desire to avoid learning for ourselves. These sources suggest rather than GenAI image generation being about learning to make art, it's instead about shortcutting the creative process of making art.

Creating art, like any other learned skill, takes time and practise to improve and perfect. Traditional and digital artists posting their carefully selected works online generally don't post their works from when they first began to create, at the messy beginning stages of, for example, poor anatomy and misunderstanding perspective. The public primarily sees the finished products after an artists' years of practise, never observing those years of awkward transition the artist had from amateur to professional. As with other areas of expertise, this can lead to the assumption that these practising artists were simply "born" with their abilities, rather than it being a result of their years of practise and dedication to their art (Helding, 2011; Howe et al., 1998). The comparison of creative outputs can lead to decreased self-confidence and self-esteem (Wijetunge et al., 2025) leading a non-artist to use GenAI technology as a means of bypassing much of the time needed to specialise in a skill (Tang et al., 2024).

Although AI companies claim that GenAI is democratizing art, the process of GenAI image outputs is more akin to a Google search than to the process of creating art. Perhaps that is enough for some people to classify as "art", and I acknowledge that art as a concept is subjective. However, I argue that if GenAI is democratizing anything it is the access to custom image creation, not art- making. I would argue that to say something "democratizes art" would be to provide greater access, both environmentally and socioeconomically, to the skills of art-making, the ability to make something with your own faculties, and the satisfaction of skill acquisition and problem solving to reach a conclusion that you are satisfied with. With GenAI image generators, most of the elements of the creative process are outsourced to a machine, making the process no more about personal art-making than it would be to commission an artwork from a practising artist – except in that case you would be supporting a human artist in the process, and may alleviate some of the environmental burden that GenAI causes (Luccioni et al., 2024; Valdivia, 2024). Writing prompts into a GenAI image generator is no more compatible with the concept of democratizing art than it is to input key terms into Google image and saving the first result.

It could be argued that a tool that does the entire process of art-making and image creation for you isn't fulfilling a desire to be better at creating art, or to develop skill in art-making. Rather, GenAI image generation is primarily fulfilling a single goal: that of having access to a custom image. To oversimplify the entire process of art-making through the use of GenAI defeats its function as a tool – that is, to aid humans to complete a particular function and aid in accessibility to that ability. Previously, AI tools built into editing software were created with the intention of helping users to complete individual tasks, not finish a project from idea to completion. For example, editing software such as Photoshop and FaceTune offer AI tools to help users perform certain actions during creation, such as identify faces to aid in the editing process, or the use of the heal brush to remove elements from an image seamlessly. These are examples of AI tools that aim to streamline the creative process without infringing on the creator's ability to control every stage of the creative process, and the current model of GenAI image generators do no fulfil that role.

On the whole, technology as a tool has consistently allowed humans to create and build in a way that surpasses all other non-human animals, with each new invention or tool being another opportunity for humans to grow and improve (Navarro and Hancock, 2023). Technology has offered a vast array of different tools to both enhance the human experience and free up more time to focus on what we believe to be important in life, such as art-making (Lawson, 2025; Navarro and Hancock, 2023). In most cases, technology offers a positive impact on our lives and its impact on art is no exception. There's no denying that technology, and more specifically the internet, has made art consumption and interaction more accessible to a greater audience (Cetinic and She, 2022; Lisney et al., 2013; Wagner, 2020). The existence of the internet has made learning about art history more accessible than ever before, with artworks that in the past were hidden behind the veil of exclusivity now available to be seen in online art galleries and museums. For the process of art-making itself, modern digital tools for art-making give a greater access to conceptualising, drawing, and artistic understanding to the masses, such as online tutorials on video sharing sites like YouTube, which provide free step-by-step instructions for materials and techniques; drawing tablets to streamline the drawing process from physical to digital with the ability to save and undo mistakes; and drawing software like Photoshop, Procreate or GIMP. These kinds of specific tools help democratize art by lowering the barrier of entry to skill accumulation and artistic knowledge, while maintaining respect and appreciation for artists and art history by making the tools useful for artists and non-artists alike.

Another concern is that with the internet being flooded with AI images, and getting progressively more lifelike and impressive each day, there is a risk that future generations could not only be influenced to use GenAI image generators instead of traditional,[10] non-AI methods, but rather could be demotivated from trying or practising any art-making at all. While there may be those who are intimidated by traditional art and the skill of artists, there are also those who are inspired by it. Most artists can attribute a certain artwork or artist that made a direct impact on their decision to pursue art and to practise art-making as a skill. Seeing an over-abundance of AI media, such as images, music, films, writing, and advertising, may discourage future generations of artists from pursuing an artistic career. The use of GenAI may become so prevalent that the need for artists could become obsolete, both due to the unmatched speed that AI can produce outputs and reduced costs. This may discourage not only new and young artists from creating art and developing the skills needed to become a skilled artist (Stueart, 2025; Zhao, 2024), but also

10 For ease of distinction, traditional in this case is including digital art made through drawing using digital software, such as photoshop or procreate, but does not include GenAI digital images.

threatens to weaken our incentive to be creative in areas not exclusive to art-making, limiting our ability for connection with other humans (Brainard, 2025). In theory, the creation of another tool that aids in creative exploration is a positive addition to the art world. However, the issue with the claims the AI companies are making is in their intentional use of "democratization". As per my conditions for legitimate democratization, for a tool to "democratize" something, it requires reducing barriers without exacerbating existing barriers, respecting the autonomy of existing participants in that activity, and allowing relevant stakeholders the opportunity to be involved in the development of the democratizing technology. However, rather than reducing barriers, GenAI instead uses artists as a means to an end and creates a new barrier between traditional artists and those using GenAI. GenAI companies don't simply desire the images from existing artists, rather they require their data to create their GenAI image outputs. Therefore, to legitimately democratize art-making would necessitate respecting the artists and involving them in the process, such as by giving proper credit and asking explicit permission for the use of their work. GenAI companies' disrespect and dismiss the autonomy of the in-group of the activity of art-making by not providing artists with an opportunity to be involved in the process, refusing to acknowledge the importance of their work when training the GenAI image models, and failing to acquire meaningful permission.

3. The Lack of Meaningful Permission

Autonomy and permission are generally considered core moral principles when it comes to mutual respect and social flourishing (Kant, 1785; Kleinig, 1982; Miller and Wertheimer, 2009). For GenAI and other areas of the internet, the concept of permission has been recommended in order to promote the welfare of both creative workers and online users (Im et al., 2021; Kyi et al., 2025, 2024). However, this recommendation has been ignored or dismissed by the companies creating the current most popular GenAI image generators. For GenAI models to make what we would classify as "art", they must be trained on art. Thus, GenAI image generators require human-created art to generate novel images, but AI companies fail to seek any permissions from the original artists whose work is being commandeered. This requirement of human-made art should necessitate the inclusion of artists in the development and design of the democratizing tool. However, in their effort to "democratize" art-making, AI companies are instead harming the current artistic community through their lack of acquiring meaningful permission from artists when using their images to train GenAI models. They use artists' creative labour as fuel for their image generators without credit, acknowledgment, or compensation.

The harm being felt by artists is multifaceted but can be summarised under what has been coined as a lack of "the three C's": permission, compensation, and credit (Chayka, 2023; Cultural Intellectual Property Rights Initiative, 2017; Kyi et al., 2025; Love, 2023). Corporations using the digital work of artists are not asking for permission to use their work; they are not compensating any artists for their labour; and they aren't crediting any artists for either their work being used either as training material or as having an impact on the hundreds of outputs produced by GenAI image generators. Companies like LAION, who are creating the enormous data sets that are being used to train GenAI image generators, collect artworks indiscriminately and thrive on high quantities of data, taking any image online that is beneficial to that end. This is done without consideration on the meanings or origins of those images and without seeking permission from the artists (Allred and Aragon, 2023; Corrall, 2024; Jiang et al., 2023; Sato, 2025; Zhang et al., 2025). The emphasis on data accumulation and quantity over quality is undercutting the artistic community, overshadowing human work and experience, and cheapening the process of art creation (Metz, 2022b).

11 It should be noted that there are artists who place less stock in the importance of authenticity and originality of an artwork, such as the practise in Eastern philosophy where creation is an act of continuous and permanent transformation (de Bucs, 2025). However, with the vast majority of images being scraped coming from western countries, seen through the white and Anglo-centric bias in the training material as explored in the previous chapter, the majority of data scraped by machine learning companies is coming from communities where the use of their work is considered "art theft" (Allred and Aragon, 2023; Goetze, 2024). This can be seen in the LAION's datasets, which are filled with

primarily English image-text pairs (Baio, 2022b), and through the numerous lawsuits coming out of the US (Cho, 2024; Vincent, 2023a, 2023b).

When training AI models, the process doesn't discriminate between images, as the only objective is extracting the highest quantity of data as possible.12 When these algorithms scrape an image from the internet, they disconnect the piece from its original intention and remove any context associated with it. This is especially harmful with art pieces, since to reduce an artwork down to its bare minimum of colour and lines denies the artist their presence within the piece, violating their autonomy by using their artwork without permission, and stripping the piece of any meaningful connections (Allred and Aragon, 2023; Ivanova, 2025; Zhang et al., 2025). To be an artist is to reveal something about the self, to translate something immaterial into reality (Heidegger, 1977; Whitehead, 2003). Artists are often deeply connected with their works, as they see their art as an extension of themselves and a form of self-expression, with the final product being an accumulation of their practise and dedication, and a show of their technical abilities (Zhang et al., 2025).

Professionally, receiving credit is considered necessary for human capital and the growing of professional reputation (Fisk, 2025). An artist's style is a fundamental property within the art space, something that is both deeply personal to the artist and generally easily identifiable by viewers (Romero, 2023). In short, regardless of the end product, whether that be fine art or fan art, the process of art-making means there is usually an intrinsic connection between the artist and their artworks. We can see this in action with the lawsuit by artists including Sarah Anderson and Karla Ortiz (Vincent, 2023a). Although their comic style layouts or style might imply a level of distance to their works due to the inherit silliness to some of the content matter, in the same way that someone making a meme may consider its creation to be trivial and inconsequential, lawsuits such as these show an inherit ownership over an artwork. An unauthorised taking of their work, regardless of the content, is a disconnection of the artist and their creations, and a violation of the

This indiscriminate scrapping of online images is also why much of the LAION datasets have been found to include real photos of children (Lavoipierre, 2024), including child sexual material (O'Brien and Hadero, 2023), and pornography (Birhane et al., 2021) core values that many artists consider paramount to their fundamental conception of autonomy and respect (Williams, 2023).

Most online artistic communities pride themselves on a system of values, primarily of being collaborative, fair, and open to sharing, networking, and supporting other artists in the community (Allred and Aragon, 2023). The methods by which GenAI image generators are trained is completely antithetical to this system of values. Artists' images are being taken without consideration of their ownership over their artworks, and their data is being used in a way that not only strips the owner of their agency over the image, but also of any meaning the original artwork once had. Collaboration is a major value within artistic communities, but many artists assert that they cannot see any meaningful way to collaborate with GenAI due to the lack of protections or assurances that their work won't be stolen by these third parties and used to produce mimicries of their work (Kawakami and Venkatagiri, 2024). The Design Inclusion Condition for GenAI image generators is thus multifaceted; it is not only necessary to allow artists involvement in the design of the tool because it will directly affect them and their livelihoods, but also necessary as a matter of ethics, as collaboration and sharing are considered pivotal to a hospitable artistic community.

Artists are hyper aware that their work is being cannibalised into outputs that could threaten their livelihoods and their communities (Akers, 2024; Babbs, 2023; Shaffi, 2023; Washburn, 2024). The unauthorised use of their creative works is causing many artists to feel that their years of learning and creative skill uptake are being undermined and exploited, all while feeling used by corporations who take their uncredited and unpaid labour to create a product that couldn't exist without the very skills the AI companies seek to "democratize". For example, Jerome Stueart, an artist from the US, notes that if mastery of a craft can come without any practice or sacrifice, then why bother struggling to create at all, writing, "what could I offer that generative AI hadn't produced in seconds" (Stueart, 2025, para. 10). Steven Zapata, a New York artist and art teacher, shares that he gets messages from students daily worrying about teaching AI systems their style before "they've had the chance to do anything good with it" (Zapata 2023, 10:37), leading to fewer artists sharing their work and engaging with artistic communities. Other artists note that GenAI reinforces the harmful narrative that making art is "easy", and therefore unworthy of being paid for their talent or labour (Shaffi, 2023).

This demoralisation of artists also harms the sense of solidarity that comes from belonging to an art community. There is an understanding between community members of the time and effort needed to accumulate their skills, and a bond over the emotional attachment to both the process of art-making and the sharing of one's work (Durán, 2019; Gemtou, 2010; Park, 2024). When GenAI hinders this process of sharing, by demoralising artists from collaboration through the non-consensual use of their work, these models deprive these communities of that solidarity. Even when an artist uses another artists' work to trace or to use as inspiration, it is an expected courtesy that they will credit the original artist when sharing their final piece. Even in stock images, artists are expected to credit the original source of an image, unless they have actively paid for the use of that image or the license agreement, a form of artistic permission, states otherwise (Adobe, 2025).

The nonconsensual taking of artists work is not limited to GenAI image generators. All artists, but especially digital artists, are likely to be subjected to art theft or impersonation at some point. The nature of digital art necessitates an understanding that anyone could save any image onto their computer to use it for whatever means they desire. Typically online artists will consider a calculation of harms when passing judgement on the unauthorised use of their work (Allred and Aragon, 2023). For example, a student using an artistic image off Google to use in an academic presentation for class would not be weighed as very harmful, and if proper credit was given then there may be no harm at all. But if a corporation used an artwork in their commercial game without credit or compensation of the original artist, for example in the case against video game company Bungie by artist Fern Hook (Phillips, 2025), then that would be considered a respect violation, amplified by the fact that a corporation is essentially "punching down" on a small creator and taking advantage of them. The Big Tech companies behind the major GenAI image generators, such as OpenAI, Midjourney, and Stable Diffusion, are identified as the latter; large scale corporations exploiting the skills and labour of small artists by automating and commodifying the act of their art production (Goetze, 2024; Ho, 2023). GenAI companies are exploitative as their GenAI image generators could not exist without the work of artists, work that is taken without permission, credit, or compensation (Kyi et al., 2025). This misuse of their artistic creations is compounded by the fact that the LAION datasets, the datasets used to train Midjourney and Stable Diffusion (and likely other AI models), are classified as being used for "research purposes" and non-commercial (Beaumont, 2022; Moody, 2024;

Vincent, 2023a). This is a loophole that benefits both LAION and the AI companies; the company compiling the data cannot be held liable for the way GenAI companies are using their datasets, and these non-profit or academic companies shield GenAI developers from accountability as they have a degree of separation from the datasets, which offers some protection against any copyright claims (Baio, 2022b). So, while artists are rightfully feeling taken advantage of through the unauthorised use of their personal works, they are met with indifference from companies who refuse to take any accountability because they weren't technically, or legally, the ones who took the data in the first place. To the extent that GenAI companies do take ownership of their unauthorised use of artists work, they hide behind the concept of the greater good and "democratizing the capacity to create", insisting that the harms being done are worth remaining competitive in the international AI race ("OpenAI—written evidence (LLM0113)," 2023). For example, OpenAI admitted that "it would be impossible to train today's leading AI models without using copyrighted materials" (Milmo, 2024, para. 5), that having an opt-out system would make the race for "democratic" AI "effectively over" (McKenzie, 2025, para. 3). Nick Clegg, Meta's former head of global affairs, emphasised this point, stating that asking artists for permission would essentially "kill the AI industry

A text and data mining (TDM) exception for copyright materials was introduced by the EU, with a narrower exception being adopted by the UK (Matulionyte, 2023). Tech companies in the US contend that using copyrighted materials for AI training falls under 'Fair Use' (Love, 2025) Japan and Singapore also have introduced variations of TDM exception for AI training (Currey et al., 2025). At the time of writing, the Australian Government appears I have definitively ruled out allowing AI companies to have any exception on the TDM of copyrighted works (Truu, 2025), suggesting that at least Australian legislation is moving towards stricter guidelines and rules to stop AI companies from indiscriminately taking works by artists without permission. overnight" (Sato, 2025, para. 4). While there is some truth in the practical difficulties of asking each artist individually for the use of their work, these statements demonstrate that rather than considering other methods to ensure the fair use of artists work for GenAI training, such as Matulionyte's (2009) proposed collecting societies, GenAI companies choose to avoid artist's input altogether, putting innovation and progress above all else, including the people necessary to its progress.

Goetze (2024) explains that while it's difficult to classify the actions of GenAI image generators as specifically art theft or plagiarism, due to the issues of style mimicry and copying not being distinctive to GenAI, GenAI are unique in that they steal labour from the artist, akin to stealing grain from a farmer to make and sell your own bread. Rather than theft, Matulionyte (2023) explains that the use of data to train GenAI could be seen in terms of moral rights violations, noting that under the Australian Copyright Act 196814 it might be possible to explained an infringement of the right to attribution and the right to integrity, but that AI companies could defend their use as "reasonable" as the industry practise of using "freely available" data online is considered the standard practice.

A common rebuttal to the discussion around the unauthorised use of an artist's work is that by putting their work online, particularly on a privately owned website such as Twitter (now X) or Instagram, the artist agrees to the terms and conditions allowing the company unfettered use of their uploaded images. The terms and conditions on privately owned websites across social media and image gallery platforms, such as DeviantArt or Photobucket, are used as a scapegoat to escape any legal or ethical responsibility for using an artist's work in any capacity without their explicit permission. The terms of use contracts on these websites are being updated regularly to reflect the emerging AI market, but consumers who have been using these platforms since they were first conceived, or even made their accounts before GenAI was even a consideration, are often considered by the private companies to have given implicit permission to the use of their images for Copyright Act 1986 Part IX, Div 2, Div 3, Div 4. means of training artificial intelligence programs, such as facial recognition or AI image generation. Despite the technology having not existed at the time of the creation of their account, platforms like Meta tend to lump in the addition of GenAI scraping with their terms of use, as the definitions are often board enough to include AI without specifically mentioning it (Phipps, 2024).

Finally, to compound this issue, Lee et al. (2025) found that LAION-5B's successor Datacomp CommonPool, contained up to 122 million samples from websites with terms of services prohibiting data scraping, with 9-13% of samples coming from sources that were copyrighted or watermarked. This shows a flaw in the "terms and conditions" rebuttal, as even on websites where the terms of services prohibit the use of data scraping, the training models continue to take data without permission, making it impossible for artists to share their work online anywhere without fear that their autonomy will be violated. Thus, GenAI image generators fail the Respecting artists' rights Condition for legitimate democratization.

4.CHAPTER ARGUMENTS FOR GENAI IMAGE GENERATORS

Amongst the defence for GenAI image generators "democratizing" art lie four reoccurring arguments. 1) That art-making is inaccessible to the average person, thus requiring the use of GenAI; 2) That artists are "gatekeeping" creativity and making it difficult for the average non-artist to engage with the traditional art community; 3) That GenAI image generators are "inspired" and "learn" as humans do, and therefore GenAI image are equivalent to human artistry; and 4) That GenAI image generators are comparable to the invention of the camera and photography, thus making the pushback a result of current artists' inability to accept technological progress. This section will explore each of these points and argue that while they raise some worthwhile issues present within art communities, they are ultimately inadequate for defending current GenAI image generators and don't justify the ethical harms being done by the technology.

4.1. "Lack of Accessibility" for Art-making

The main argument that GenAI image generators are democratizing art comes from the idea that art-making is inaccessible to the average person based on the perceived requirement of expertise, including the training time and connections required to obtain that expertise, and expensive equipment (Duggal, 2024; Othman, 2024; Park, 2024; Ramos, 2024; Tuisk, 2023). On this definition of accessibility, the defenders of GenAI image generators are primarily referring to access to a particular skillset (Kelley, 2022; Merchant, 2025a; Seger et al., 2023). Therefore, to democratize art is to make artistic creation accessible to a broader audience, not just for artists who already have the required skills or formal training but for everyone. By this account, anyone who has access to a computer can now have the ability to create whatever art they desire (within the constraints of the technology itself), with some arguing that the process results in greater creative outcomes due to its detachment from the traditional subjectivity associated with art (Park, 2024, p. 6). The primary rebuttal to this argument is that art has always been democratic, at least to some degree. There has rarely been a time when making art and creative expression haven't been available to (almost) everyone in some form. That's not to say that there isn't an element of truth to the idea that skill uptake can often be costly, both monetarily and in the time required to learn a new skill. An economic advantage will be beneficial when developing any new skill, as access to the means to supply yourself with higher quality equipment and in-depth instruction will always aid in the ease of skill uptake. Being able to both support yourself economically while also having the free time and energy outside work to practise are clearly important. However, unlike some other skills that require expensive equipment or academic knowledge to peruse, creativity is one of the few human exports that can be practised (in many cases) without access to any expensive materials or high-quality machinery. Admittedly, there are some artistic endeavours that require more specialise gear than others, such as filmmaking and photography. However, at the ground

level, meaning that of simply creating something, the people who have access to GenAI image generator technology also have the means to create art by other avenues (or at the very least attempt to make art).15 This low barrier to entry is especially true of digital art, where individuals have access to not only programs that enable them to draw and create on their computer, but also to the plethora of information made available online for free by other artists. When it comes to art-making, authors such as Allred and Aragon (2023) argue that digital art is one of the most accessible16 forms of art in history, explaining that online art communities have an emphasis on collaboration and participation, where the sharing of creative information and the support of other artists is integral to the ecosystem of digital art spaces. For art consumption, the combination of digitised art collections from art galleries and the ongoing creation of new digital art improves accessibility to art by increasing the capacity for more people to engage with it through the reduction of barriers to participation (Enhuber, 2015). Traditional art can have physical barriers, in that it requires a physical embodiment of an idea for it to be appreciated and viewing it in person is argued as often being necessary to fully appreciate it. However digital art transcends the requirement of this physical form. Digital art is shared at its most authentic as a digital, reproduceable image.17 This enables those who may not have access to traditional art, either financially, geographically or physically, to participate in art culture and community from their home.

When considering the traditional definition of "accessibility", the online art community generally advocates for accessibility accommodations for those with disabilities or lower socioeconomic situations. For example, with the creation of cheap art software for creating art, This isn't to dismiss that many avenues of art-making do require special equipment or knowledge to create effectively, but rather to demonstrate that from the beginner's level, most art forms have some method of creating that is cost effective. For example, although filmmaking requires certain technologies to create, such as a camera and editing software, the beginner level of filmmaking, such as with a mobile phone and free software, is no higher than what is being claimed is accessible about GenAI image generation.

In this case "accessible" is primarily referring to "the most accessible" as well as its accessibility to those with disabilities, as many of the tools that make computers accessible can also aid in the digital creation of art. 17 The authenticity would depend on the resolution of the viewers screen, of course. If a digital image is intended to be viewed on a high-resolution computer screen, then viewing it on a phone screen may limit the appreciation of the image. such as GIMP or Procreate, or the publishing of free online tutorials and information. The tech companies that are developing GenAI image generators claim that they are another tool for accessibility, however their actions are undermined by the parasitic nature the technology has with pre-existing accessibility tools. For example, a modern accessibility tool for the visual impaired is the creation of alternative-text (alt-text), a text descriptor that's attached to a digital image explaining in detail what an image contains that can serve as a substitute for images when they fail to load, or for reading software to pick up and describe for the visually impaired. It also improves search engine optimisation and makes it easier for people to find certain images online, making it a tool that improves access both in finding images and for more people to view and understand them (accessiBe, 2025).

Many artists will use alt-text when uploading their images and artworks online in an effort to improve accessibility and interactions with their work. However, these alt-text descriptors are exploited by GenAI companies and used to train datasets for GenAI image generators, effectively using the artists' attempt at improving accessibility against them as their alt-text additions make it easier for image datasets to scrape their works. For example, this is the case for the digital artist Greg Rutkowski, a digital fantasy artist whose name is one of the most used prompts in current GenAI image generators (Heikkilä, 2022b; Hutchinson and John, 2023). Rutkowski's work and style are some of the easiest to replicate due to his consideration for adding extensive alt-text to all his online artworks (Allred and Aragon, 2023; Heikkilä, 2022b).

Those defending GenAI image generators claim that current art communities lack tools for inclusion and actively exclude people from access to art-making through gatekeeping art (Lafae, 2022). However, in an effort to improve accessibility to art-making, GenAI image generators are systematically harming those within the online art community, such as Rutkowski, who are already making prosocial efforts to make their work more accessible. This can have the knock on effect of effectively punishing them for trying to creating a more hospitable online creative space and causing them to become frustrated as they notice a drop in interest for their work-for-hire art (Goetze, 2024; Hutchinson and John, 2023; Petrick, 2024). The companies making current GenAI image models directly benefit from artists who are using tools to make the space more accessible but fail to acknowledge these efforts, and in some cases dismiss them entirely (Crabapple, 2023). This is one example where GenAI as an "accessibility tool" forgoes considering those that accessibility was originally spearheaded for. Instead, these tech companies are concerned with appearing to champion accessibility and taking credit for making art more inclusive while benefiting from the accessibility tools already being used freely by practising artists.

Finally, even if we consider GenAI as a tool for affordability rather than accessibility, considering the necessitation's to having access to a computer, the internet, payment for full access to the product and at least some operational understanding of the tool, the technology lacks the universality that it claims (Bak Herrie et al., 2025). GenAI image generators require socioeconomic status and technological understanding similar to that of traditional art-making (and potentially even more so when you consider that a beginner artist could begin learning with cheap materials such as a pencil and paper). But say we focus on one of the core arguments from GenAI companies, that being the inability to learn a new skill because of a lack of time due to work obligations (Salkowitz, 2022). Trying to solve the issue of the general population lacking the time to properly dedicate themselves to a craft because of the demand of their labour in the capitalist market with the capitalist solution of automating the art-making process is a band-aid solution and appears counter intuitive. The concept of "democratizing" art through the use of GenAI fails to address the underlying societal roadblocks preventing those who would like to pursue artistic ventures from having the time and resources to practise art-making. It is a surface level solution that lacks the depth required to be a permanent fix for the perceived lack of accessibility to art-making.

4.2. Artistic "Gatekeeping"

A reoccurring topic of discussion around GenAI image generation is the idea that artists gatekeep art by "hoarding" all the skill and talent for themselves, making it difficult or inhospitable for the average person to explore their creativity and create their own art (Magni et al., 2024; Park, 2024). This understanding of the elitism and gatekeeping within art is not without merit. Historically, the church was responsible for the vast majority of art commissions, intrinsically tying art to the religious elite to represent the power of the church (Belting, 1994). This elitism within the art world further emphasised the imbalance of power between the upper echelons and the working class (Park, 2024). Over the last century, the narrative of art elitism was perpetuated by art galleries and museums, who amassed their collections via the wealth of rich benefactors which in turn discouraged public participation (David, 1999). In modern art-making, there is a tendency for some artists to believe that some level of elitism is beneficial to art-making, as it ensures a certain standard of art excellence (Smith, 1986). Beginning from the patronage during the renaissance period, the education and the resources required to be classified as an "artist" could be difficult to access by the average person (Barzun, 1987).

However, this conception of the "high art" artist (Golitsyn, 2000) is identifiably white and Eurocentric. To only think of art under this lens of being exclusively for the rich or affluent discounts the years of art-making by other cultures and peoples (Araeen, 2024), thereby perpetuating the very imbalance of power that the "democratization" of art seeks to address. When considering making art more accessible, we need to be considering those outside of the white, Eurocentric bubble, as discussed in the previous chapter of this book, that GenAI data seems to allude to. Labelling the anti-AI traditional artists as 'elitist' not only discounts the years of work that most artists commit to in order to improve their craft, but also the artists who are underrepresented by the internet and social media (Topaz et al., 2022).

Under a Western viewpoint, traditional art education has identified the artist predominantly as a "White male genius", with authors such as Travis (2019, p. 96) noting that these "conceptualizations of the arts and artists solidify the idea that the arts are the purview of the elite and the so-called talented perpetuating exclusion of others". This perpetuation informs the way the pro-AI image creators view traditional art-making, leading them to believe that most, if not all,

traditional art-making is elitist (Białkowski, 2024; Masley, 2025). When being dismissed by practising traditional artists, GenAI image creators could feel legitimised as they aren't falling into the "elitist trap", thereby disregarding any valid concerns raised by anti-AI artists. This argument is amplified by the media, with people such as the Stability.ai CEO Emad Mostaque being quoted stating that artists want to "keep their monopoly on visual communication" and wrongly attributing artists as "arguing for skill segregation" (Crabapple, 2023).18 Similar to the argument point regarding lack of accessibility, this is a misinterpretation based on the narrow view that creativity and art-making are only possible when one has access to certain tools or is born with a certain skill. This not only discourages novices from experimenting with art-making, damaging their self- esteem when they are not immediately good at creating, but also delegitimises those who have spent years practising and learning to acquire and maintain their skills (Helding, 2011).

The concept of an artistic "genius" (Travis, 2019, p. 96) also sets the precedent that people are born with their skill, rather than acquiring it. There are studies that suggest that while it can be beneficial for someone to have a disposition towards creativity, ultimately the interpretation of "innate skills" is a myth, and that any talent that was perceived as being innate in the individual could be explained via other means, such as intensive training or a particular upbringing that valued creativity (Helding, 2011; Howe et al., 1998). It could be argued that there are those better equipped, whether that's physically or mentally, to excel at art-making within society. However, while there is research to suggest this may be true of many athletic abilities (Baker and Wattie, 2018), art-making and creativity has been shown as one of the few human abilities that can be developed regardless of nature born skill (Horns, 1939). Therefore, rather than their claim of improving access to creativity, the perpetuation of artistic gatekeeping and of the "artists vs non- artists" rhetoric by GenAI companies risks pushing people away from engaging with art communities or participating in traditional art-making practises.

These statements seem ironic when you consider that the businesses creating these image generation models are monopolising power among only a few corporations and attempting to segregate artists from the public through alienation (Jiang et al., 2023).

The act of voicing concerns about GenAI images can in itself be interpreted as a form of elitism within the pro-AI space, with traditional artists being referred to as elitist when explaining the unethical qualities of the emerging technology (Lafae, 2022). Some defenders of GenAI proclaim it as a tool that challenges the status quo and that “challenges traditional gatekeeping in the art world” (Park, 2024, p. 6). Artists that express hurt over GenAI are being told to “move forward rather than sulking about it” (Metz, 2022a, para. 16) and that voicing any concerns with these models is demonstrating a “paternalistic silliness”, thereby devaluing the anti-AI artist to someone that “doesn’t trust people or society” (Heikkilä, 2022a, para. 12). These reductive arguments fail to acknowledge that many artists are not combative to the idea of making art more accessible, and are often not intentionally gatekeeping art-making, but rather are opposed to the means by which GenAI incorrectly claims to be a tool that is democratizing art-making and creativity.

4.3. The Way GenAI Image Generators “Learn”

Another defence of the way in which GenAI image generators work is the idea that they “learn” in the same way that humans do; by looking at existing works, taking elements and “remixing” them to create a novel art piece (Masood, 2025). Some GenAI image defenders anthropomorphise GenAI image generators, claiming that they are ‘inspired’ in the same way human artists are. This argument may hold some merit when it comes to discussing the copyright law around GenAI generated images, as there is a slippery slope when trying to copyright a ‘style’ of work. Humans do imitate styles, especially when first learning their craft as a form of practise, so this could lead to an uncertain legal battlefield for human artists to contend with (Shoemaker, 2024). However, these discussions on inspiration derail the valid critiques people have about the unethical attributes of the tech companies and instead place the onus of blame on the AI itself, portraying it as an autonomous being (Jiang et al., 2023).

One rebuttal against this claim is that GenAI is not autonomous. Brainard (2023) explains that AI lacks the capacity to be creative as it cannot satisfy the conditions of having autonomy or curiosity that are necessary for claims of inspiration, thereby making it a mistake to attribute human creativity to, or to anthropomorphise, AI. GenAI image generators require prompts from human users and creates a result that is statistically the best fit. GenAI is no more inspired than a calculator is inspired. But even if we could accept that GenAI was "inspired" in some way, it would still not be inspired in the way humans are. The "inspiration" argument fails to recognise two key differences between a human artist and a machine; that of the sheer volume of work produced and the extreme difference in time it takes to produce a finished image. Making the claim that humans, like GenAI, copy other artists styles and borrow from other artists is not an accurate comparison. A human artist would need years of practise to properly replicate the style of another artist, especially with any degree of perfect replication, let alone being able to reproduce the style of any artist who has posted their work online (Rizzi, 2023). This is not just due to the difficulty a human would have in producing a perfectly replicated artwork,19 but also because even if a human were able to make perfect copies, that would still only be a single person doing a few artworks. Necessary time and effort are needed to organically produce convincing counterfeits, so the harm to the original artist is lessened based on the quantity of original counterfeits that are being made available online.

The main issue, or rather the issue that is unique to GenAI and machine learning (ML) images, is the quantity of images that these programs are able to create, and the complete saturation the market (Jiang et al., 2023; Ortiz, 2022). The speed and scale that GenAI image generators both collect data and create new outputs is unfathomable by human standards of creation, thereby creating a proliferation of images that can suffocate human competition (Goetze, 2024). Furthermore, when a prompter is asking for a GenAI image "in the style of" another artist, for example the previously mentioned Rutkowski, they aren't asking the model to be inspired by the

This could also be seen as a valid skill, even if the outcome of the work was ethically dubious – for example the Chinese artists who are paid to perfectly replicate artworks to be sold cheap as imitations ae seen as artists in their own right due to the technical abilities that they have (de Bucs, 2025; Rao, 2014) artist, they are asking it to replicate their style as a means of having a custom image from that artist for themselves without engaging with the original artist or supporting them financially. From an economic standpoint, employers tend to favour lower costs and higher outputs, resulting in many professional artists, such as concept artists and illustrators, being sidelined due to their inability to compete with GenAI (Merchant, 2025b; Zhao, 2024). This has caused many artists to consider changing careers entirely to fields that are less impacted by AI, including leaving their creative fields entirely (Kawakami and Venkatagiri, 2024). GenAI technology overwhelms the market with images created through the use of artists' data, pushing those same artists out of the market and making it impossible for them to keep up with the ever-increasing demand set by GenAI. This in turn replaces them in the same market and centralises the power within the market between only a few corporations (Jiang et al., 2023).

Ultimately, the harm from GenAI comes down to quantity. Those who aren't artists, don't plan on commissioning an artist, or aren't connected to the 'art world', may have the intuition that the issues surround AI image generators doesn't affect or concern them. Individuals who are only interested in seeing a simple image come to life or who need a quick, custom image for their school or work presentation will presumably not see the use of GenAI image generators as having an impact on their lives, or the lives of others. If they weren't going to pay an artist anyway, then they are not taking anything financially from them, they may counter. And on a surface level, they're correct; one person using an image generator a couple of times will not cause massive damage to the art community, or to society, or to the environment. But the dose makes the poison, and with 125 million active users and the 114 million images that Canva estimated in 2023 had been generated using Stable Diffusion (Nicoletti & Bass 2023), the growing user base of GenAI image generators creates a quantity of images that human artists can't compete with, and that even the most casual of GenAI user shouldn't ignore.

Additionally, even if GenAI were capable of engaging in creativity or learn in the same way humans do, the ethical issues present in how they are trained would still remain active.

4.4. Comparison to Photography

A reoccurring argument for the permissibility of GenAI image generators is that the disruption they are causing to the art community is similar, if the not the same, as the disruptions caused by previous technological advancements, such as photography (Ivanova, 2025; Park, 2024; Petrick, 2024). The argument contends that just as photography gave rise to new forms of art and "liberated" painting from realism (Epstein and Hertzmann, 2023, p. 1110) and "stimulated an artistic revolution" (Petrick, 2024, para. 4), GenAI image generators offer the same opportunity to explore new aesthetic possibilities and pushes the boundaries of artistic expression. On the surface these technologies appear to be replicating a similar evolution of the artistic landscape. For example, with the disruption to jobs and opportunities being similar talking points during both transitions, and a comparison of the "pushing a button" of photography with "making a prompt" of GenAI images.

Photography was also seen as a way to "democratize" portrait and landscape painting, where those lacking the technical skills to produce highly realistic paintings of people or environments now being able to capture those moments in real time using a machine (Petrick, 2024). It is an understandable comparison to make.

However, there is one dramatic difference between the harm of GenAI image generation compared to other endeavours, such as photography; no previous artistic technology has required the copyright violation of existing and deceased artists' work to make the new technology function (Epstein et al., 2023; Hulick, 2024b). No other previous "disruption" to the art world has had the potential to cause this huge of a quantity of harm, not only because of the harm to practising artists, but also due to globalisation and the environmental factors of the technology. Watkins (2025, para. 12), noting a connection between AI aesthetics and fascism, explains that "no matter how deeply avant-garde art has engaged in shock and putative nihilism, no artist...has ever made art with the sole aim of harming the already vulnerable". While this is an uncharitable conception of AI, as GenAI companies didn't set out with the sole aim of harming the already vulnerable, I would argue that GenAI technology harms artists and vulnerable groups in a way that is unfathomable through any other pre-existing medium, including photography.

As GenAI image generators can create outputs at a speed completely unreproducible by any human being, it is an unfair comparison with photography (Goetze, 2024). While photography had the inevitable side effect of putting some portrait and landscape painters out of their work, it didn't harm the vulnerable or marginalised groups in society through its creation or use, either intentionally or as a side effect of its creation. At the time it was only the elite who were able to afford paintings of themselves, so the introduction of photography opened up an avenue for those outside of the upper classes to procure images of themselves and of the world around them (Hertzmann, 2022). A similar argument has been made for how GenAI has given the average person access to custom aesthetic images as a way to combat the elitism and gatekeeping present in artistic communities.

Although there is some truth in that the history of elitism within the art world somewhat continues to permeate into modern discourse, the gatekeeping in the past is far less prevalent now than before, particularly in 1826 when photography was first introduced (Wright, 2023). The barriers to entry into the art community are arguably the lowest they've ever been. The internet gives access to a plethora of information and tutorials that were completely unheard of at the creation of photography, thereby giving access and "democratizing" art-making through information and advanced tools. While on the surface it appears that GenAI image generators are comparable to the invention of photography, GenAI, in its current form, causes more avoidable harm than any other previous artform. Photography was able to aid in reducing barriers to a form of art-making without creating new systemic exclusions, and it was able to do so without using uncredited artists' pre-existing work to train the new technology. GenAI image generators fail on both these counts, making the comparison ultimately misguided.

5. CHAPTER CONCLUSION

In this chapter, it has been argued that Generative AI image tools fail to meet both the Respecting artists' rights Condition and the Design Inclusion Condition, which are essential for any claim of legitimate democratization. A truly democratizing system must respect the rights, permission, and agency of those already participating in the field. However, instead of supporting artists, these technologies often overlook them — or worse, exploit their work without meaningful acknowledgment.

Artists have long operated within a culture that values collaboration, fairness, and the open exchange of ideas. In contrast, Generative AI systems frequently operate in opposition to these principles. By separating artworks from their creators and using them as training material without permission, credit, or compensation, these systems disrupt the relationship between the artist and their work. This disconnection is not merely technical — it is deeply ethical, as it reduces creative expression to data while stripping it of its original meaning and intent.

The chapter also critically understandd several common arguments used to defend the rise of Generative AI image tools. One such claim is that art-making has traditionally been inaccessible, and that artists act as "gatekeepers" of creativity. However, this perspective overlooks the growing presence of collaborative communities, open learning platforms, and freely accessible resources that already support creative participation. The idea of widespread exclusion, in this sense, is often overstated.

Another argument suggests that AI systems are "inspired" in a way similar to human artists. This chapter challenges that comparison, emphasizing that human creativity is shaped by lived experience, intention, and emotional depth — qualities that cannot be replicated through data-driven processes. Additionally, the sheer scale at which AI systems can produce images introduces further concerns, as it shifts the balance of creative production in ways that may disadvantage human creators.

Finally, while comparisons are sometimes drawn between Generative AI and earlier technologies such as photography, this chapter highlights important differences. Although both involve technological mediation, the moral effects are not the same. The manner in which Generative AI systems are trained, and the impact they have on artists and vulnerable communities, raises concerns that go beyond those associated with earlier creative tools.

Taken together, these arguments reinforce a central conclusion: Generative AI image tools, in their current form, do not meet the conditions required for true democratization. Rather than supporting a fair, respectful, and inclusive creative environment, they risk undermining the very principles they claim to promote.

Chapter 4: Conclusion

This book has argued that when Generative AI companies claim to be "democratizing" art, such a claim must be judged against clear and meaningful standards. To assess this, three essential conditions were explaineded: fair accessibility, respect for autonomy, and design inclusion. These principles form the minimum requirements for any tool or technology to be considered genuinely democratizing.

Throughout this discussion, the workings of Generative AI image systems have been understandd, along with the ways in which these technologies are presented to the public. It has been shown that AI companies frequently promote their tools as making art more accessible and inclusive. However, when these claims are tested against the defined framework, significant shortcomings become evident.

Under the Fair Accessibility Condition, it was argued that true democratization requires reducing barriers without reinforcing or creating new forms of exclusion. In practice, however, Generative AI systems often replicate and amplify existing societal biases — particularly those related to race, gender, and disability. Instead of fostering inclusive participation, these systems risk reinforcing stereotypes and deepening inequalities. Furthermore, while accessibility is often highlighted as a key benefit, there is a lack of meaningful consideration for disabled communities. In many cases, existing accessibility tools and ideas are repurposed without genuine engagement with the communities they are meant to serve. As a result, the promise of accessibility remains incomplete.

The Respecting artists' rights Condition highlights another critical failure. While Generative AI is often framed as a tool that enhances creativity, it does so at the expense of the very artists whose work enables its existence. By using artistic content without proper permission, recognition, or compensation, these systems undermine the autonomy of creators. This not only raises ethical concerns but also affects artists emotionally and financially. More broadly, it risks discouraging emerging artists from participating in creative spaces, weakening the very community that sustains artistic practice.

The Design Inclusion Condition further reveals the limitations of these technologies. A genuinely democratizing system must involve relevant stakeholders in its development, particularly those who are directly affected by it. However, many Generative AI tools have been developed and deployed without meaningful input from artists or marginalized communities. This lack of inclusion leads to systems that fail to account for potential harms and overlook the needs of those they claim to serve.

Taken together, these findings demonstrate that Generative AI image tools, in their current form, do not meet the conditions required for legitimate democratization. As a result, the widespread claim that these technologies are "democratizing art" is not only incomplete but also misleading.

Even beyond the question of democratization, these conditions highlight broader ethical responsibilities. A technology that fails to ensure fairness and respect cannot be considered ethically sound, regardless of its intended purpose. When such a technology is promoted as democratizing, despite failing to meet these standards, it becomes doubly problematic — both in its impact and in its representation.

This does not mean that Generative AI lacks potential. With thoughtful design, ethical consideration, and meaningful inclusion of stakeholders, it could evolve into a tool that genuinely supports accessibility and creative participation. However, in its current state, it lacks the ethical foundation necessary to fulfill that promise.

For Generative AI to move toward true democratization, it must begin by addressing the concerns of those most affected — particularly marginalized communities and the artists whose work forms the backbone of these systems. Only then can it be considered a tool that not only expands access, but does so in a way that is fair, respectful, and genuinely inclusive.

The moral effects of Generative AI within the art world remain complex, dynamic, and continually evolving. As these technologies become more deeply integrated into everyday life, the need for critical and ethical reflection becomes increasingly important. This work has aimed to contribute to that growing conversation by highlighting key concerns surrounding fairness, autonomy, and inclusion in the context of AI-driven creativity.

At the same time, it is important to acknowledge that this discussion is not exhaustive. Several significant areas related to AI ethics extend beyond the scope of this book and deserve further exploration.

One such area is the environmental impact of Generative AI. The development and operation of these systems require substantial computational resources, leading to high levels of energy and water consumption. These factors carry not only environmental consequences but also financial and social implications, affecting communities in ways that are often overlooked. A deeper examination of sustainability and environmental responsibility in AI development is therefore essential.

Another important dimension involves issues of labour and exploitation. The creation and maintenance of AI systems often rely on unseen human labor, including data annotation and content moderation. Questions around fairness, compensation, and working conditions in these processes raise serious ethical concerns that warrant closer attention.

Closely related is the concept of data colonialism, where data is extracted from individuals and communities — often without meaningful permission — and used to develop technologies that primarily benefit large organizations. Understanding how biased training data intersects with these broader power dynamics is crucial for evaluating the ethical foundations of AI systems.

Additionally, longstanding philosophical debates — such as the definition of art, and whether AI can truly be considered creative — have been intentionally set aside in this discussion. While these questions are deeply relevant, they represent a distinct line of inquiry that requires its own dedicated exploration.

Looking ahead, as regulatory frameworks begin to evolve and efforts are made to make AI training practices more ethical, new questions will inevitably arise. In particular, if the ethical concerns surrounding data use and permission are addressed, the conversation may shift toward more fundamental questions: What does it mean for an AI to be an artist? And how should creativity itself be understood in a world where machines can generate complex and compelling visual outputs?

These questions signal that the discussion is far from over. Rather, it is entering a new phase — one that will continue to challenge our understanding of creativity, ownership, and ethics in the age of artificial intelligence.

www.ingramcontent.com/pod-product-compliance
Lightning Source LLC
Chambersburg PA
CBHW071357230926
51846CB00002B/582
* 9 7 8 4 4 7 8 9 3 7 1 9 8 *